Graham Sharpe is Media Relations Manager for the William Hill Organization, having let loose on the British public some of the wackier bets of recent times. He was born and bred in Harrow, Middlesex, where he now lives with his wife and two sons. He is a great fan of pop music of the mid-sixties, and used to run an elite and enlightened fan club of twenty-eight members for the McCoys. Another hobby is football, and besides supporting Luton Town and Wealdstone FC (and enduring crises when they occasionally play each other), he currently stars in Hatch End FC as Manager and player.

Graham Sharpe

RARE
STAKES

ILLUSTRATIONS BY
Bill Tidy

A Pan Original

PAN BOOKS · LONDON AND SYDNEY

To . . . Sheila, Steeven, Paul and Brooksie . . . my inspiration

First published 1986 by Pan Books Ltd,
Cavaye Place, London SW10 9PG
9 8 7 6 5 4 3 2 1
© Graham Sharpe 1986
Illustrations © Bill Tidy 1986
ISBN 0 330 29632 9
Photoset by Parker Typesetting Service, Leicester
Printed and bound in Great Britain by
Cox & Wyman Ltd, Reading

Every effort has been made to contact copyright holders.
In the event of an inadvertent omission or error, the author
should be notified
c/o Pan Books Ltd, 18–21 Cavaye Place,
London SW10 9PG

INTRODUCTION

*'I've been a gambler all my life. It separates the winners
from the losers, and that's the excitement. Like you can go
out to Las Vegas in a $45,000 Cadillac – and go home in
a $7,500 bus that isn't yours! That's how dangerous the
table is. But if you can go up there and challenge it you
can go away a tremendous winner.'*
RYAN O'NEAL (ACTOR)

*'You don't gamble to win – you gamble so you can gamble
the next day.'*
BERT AMBROSE (BAND LEADER)

I think I finally realized for sure that a large percentage of
the world's population is gambling mad when I witnessed
at first hand the amazing phenomenon of apparently sane
people handing over good cash in the hope of winning
more by betting on a fictional event, the outcome of which
was entirely down to the whims of the script-writers of a
TV show.

Of course, the event in question was the notorious 'Who
Shot J.R.?' episode of the staggeringly successful *Dallas*
series, and I'm afraid I was the person responsible for
causing the outbreak of J.R. betting fever which eventually
resulted in the best part of a quarter of a million pounds
changing hands.

It is part of my job, as a member of the publicity department for the bookies William Hill, to encourage the public
to wager on events as unlikely as the capture of the Loch
Ness Monster, or as unpredictable as the sex and name of
the next royal baby.

But one day I was mooching around, thinking of not very
much, when my wife, Sheila, happened to remark, 'It could

◇ 5 ◇

be anyone.' Now, I'm used to her making apparently meaningless remarks at various times – 'I do' was one of her best – but this particular gem just appeared out of the blue. 'What could be anyone?' I enquired. 'The person who's going to shoot J.R.,' she said. At the time I was not an avid watcher of *Dallas*, but as Sheila began to elaborate on the number of people who were in a position to carry out the imminent shooting of this fictitious character, I became more and more interested. She was putting forward a seemingly endless list of suspects – all of whom had every good reason in the world to assist J.R. Ewing, oil baron and all-round bad guy, to shuffle off this mortal coil. And what's more, my wife's interest in who would do the dastardly deed was, I quickly realized, apparently shared by ninety-nine per cent of the country.

An enquiry from Richard Moore of the *Sunday Mirror* newspaper as to whether we would be issuing any odds about the shooting finally convinced me to take my courage in both hands and go and ask one of my directors whether I could have permission to bet on a pre-ordained event, over which we had no control whatsoever, and what's more, didn't even involve real people.

Wary of the reaction I would encounter, I'd already taken the precaution of ringing round some of Fleet Street's most respected TV critics and mentioning just what I was considering. Their answers were at first unanimous: 'Under no circumstances should you do that – because I happen to know whodunnit.' Then they all proceeded to give me a completely different answer!

This gave me the confidence to put forward the idea; if the sages of Fleet Street didn't know, then I was convinced no one else did.

After much persuasion the idea was given the go-ahead and I compiled a list of suspects and their odds, released them to the press and sat back to await the reaction.

It was immediate and stunning. The *Sunday Mirror* was the first paper to publish the betting. Within hours of the news breaking, the media went wild for the story. First to

pick up on it were the BBC themselves, who announced the betting on the *Grandstand* programme!

The following day all the tabloid national newspapers were full of it. Even the BBC's racing coverage had jockey-turned-commentator Jimmy Lindley telling viewers that when he had asked somebody in the paddock about the decision of Lester Piggott to ride a certain horse in the Derby, all he got in reply was, 'Tell me why the only thing anyone wants to bet on is Who Shot J.R.?' There was a filmed report and interview about the bet in BBC TV News, and virtually all the country's radio stations carried items.

Throughout the day leading up to the screening of the vital episode, betting shop tills were ringing with the sound of cash pouring in from punters who would normally only ever risk a bet on the Grand National or the Derby, and by the time the dramatic programme was shown, over £100,000 had poured into William Hill's coffers.

The audience which sat down to watch was estimated at over twenty million in the UK alone. They saw J.R. working on his own in the office at night. He heard a noise, called out 'Who's there?' and crossed the room to find out. Two shots rang out – and the credits rolled. Ten minutes later it was being shown in 'action replay' on BBC News, which flashed up the latest betting odds on to the screen.

The next day the money continued to roll in as people put forward their own theories. A man rang me to say, 'I think the gun was in a coat, hanging on a stand, which then fell down causing the gun to fire.' 'Yes,' I said, 'nice theory, but there were two shots.' There was a short silence. Then – 'It bounced!'

Another client asked for a price against the Mafia having carried out the killing. And a member of the SAS rang up Terry Wogan (who was himself a 1000/1 shot in the betting due to his passionate love of the programme!) to deny that they had been sent in to eliminate J.R.

By the time the next series of the show began and it was revealed that second-favourite Kristin was the guilty party, we'd taken nearly £200,000.

Some ten years ago I realized that the weather would be an ideal topic to bet on – after all, even those punters who are convinced the bookies rig the results of everything from Miss World to the Derby could hardly accuse them of influencing the weather, could they?

With the British loving nothing more than a chat about the current state of the climate and how it is too hot or too cold or too wet or too dry, I tentatively tried out weather-betting by offering a price against snow falling on the roof of the London Weather Centre at any time during the twenty-four hours of Christmas Day.

The bet proved phenomenally successful and we took a great deal of money – and have done every year since. We've also won every single penny staked, for it hasn't snowed on the roof of the Weather Centre on Christmas Day for a dozen years now.

In complete contrast, 1976 saw the UK sweltering in the hottest summer for years. It hadn't rained in London for a couple of weeks. 'How long can it last?' we wondered, and then asked punters to tell us, offering them odds of 5/1 against predicting the day on which the drought would end.

And then two years later, we were enduring one of the wettest summers on record – and we had to ask punters to predict a dry spell. The story made the front page of the country's two top-selling newspapers on 9 August 1978: 'Betcha It Won't Rain' screamed the headline in the *Sun*, and 'Sodden Awful – Fancy a Flutter on the First Dry Spell?' asked the *Mirror*.

Since those early days we've had all sorts of fun with the weather – and so have our punters. I've offered odds on the highest temperatures, lowest temperatures, the length of wet and dry spells, put up a price against it raining for forty days and forty nights following a wet St Swithins and even offered a price against it raining on the day Prince Charles and Princess Diana got married. Now, on *this* bet I thought people betting on a dry day were on a real certainty – surely there was no way it would be ALLOWED to rain even one small drop on that day of all days! And it didn't.

So, if people will bet on TV soap operas and the vagaries of the notoriously fickle British climactic conditions, there is surely no limit to the things which will encourage them to have a little flutter – or even a large one.

And if you read on, you'll discover just how true that is . . .

Graham Sharpe

26. August 1984

Dear Sir,

I am writing to you because I believe you are the leading book makers in the country, and there is no branch in Wigan.

Can you arrange for me to have a "flutter" on the following. I would like to take a chance that eventually all the first forenames of Prince Charles and Princess Diana's children will spell WALES. I do not mean they will necessarily be born in that order.

Is it possible for you to arrange me some odds.

Yours sincerely & thank you

Hard to swallow

When the runner he had backed barely maintained a snail's pace during the race, the irate punter was not amused – he ate the offending competitor.

Which just happened to be a slug.

Outsider Whisky Galore had just won the exciting Guinness Slug Stakes, organized to raise cash for charity. Seven slugs had sprinted flat out for an hour and a half and judge Chris Bruce was devastated that his selection, Alfred the Great, a hot favourite, was beaten.

Said Chris, 'I'd put a lot of money on Alfred the Great – seventy-five pence, in fact!'

Professional actor Chris, whose CB codename is The Executioner (aptly enough), added, 'The creature just slid down, the barmaid nearly fainted and Whisky Galore's owner just couldn't believe it.

'There was no immediate effect on me – but I felt a bit sluggish the next morning.'

Beau's Bath bet

A contemporary report from the mid-eighteenth century records an out-of-the-ordinary wager. 'Because Beau Nash had bet that he could, a man ran himself to death to make the journey from Bath to London and back within a specified time.'

Callous? Yes, but there was a 'happy ending'. 'Whereupon Nash took up a collection at the Rooms for the benefit of the widow.'

I notice he didn't compensate her out of his own winnings.

Bet balls up

Policemen in Hull couldn't believe their eyes when four naked lads stumbled into the station late one night – with their private parts tied together with string.

The four explained that they had done it to win a bet on a night out – but the knots had become too tight to undo. The policemen, reported the *Sun* newspaper, came to the rescue of the highly strung friends.

Death watch

The Indian rickshaw puller and municipal worker each coveted the other's wrist-watch. So they agreed on a bet: they would have a spirit-drinking competition, the stakes to be the cost of the bill and the loser's watch.

The bet was struck in Warangal, South East India, in January 1986 – and both men drank themselves to death.

Pat's peach of a bet

Liverpool bookie Pat Whelan came up with a peach of a bet for clients when the Queen opened Liverpool's International Flower Festival in 1984 – Pat offered odds on the colour of her hat!

Peach was made 12/1 favourite with khaki the complete outsider at 1000/1. In the event apple green at 33/1 proved to be the winner.

Whelan still takes a few pounds each year offering 50/1 against Lord Lucan turning up alive within twelve months of bets being staked.

Betting Beatles

The Beatles lost a case of champagne in the early days of their career to rival group Rory Storm and the Hurricanes, according to their manager at the time, Alan Williams.

Both bands were playing in Hamburg in the early sixties. They struck a wager as to which of them could whip up such a storm whilst playing that they would smash up the stage floor of the club in which they were appearing.

Lennon, McCartney and co. finally lost out to Storm, but when the club owner found out about the bet he was not amused, and sent off a squad of heavies to sort the two groups out.

Dear Sirs,

Would you accept a bet and offer me the odds @ 30p per bet on the following bets :—

1. Before the turn of the 20th Century: it will be generally assumed that God has intervened to stop a 3rd World War.

2. There will be an extraordinary number of reports of U.F.O. landings on Earth.

3. An extraordinary number of children will develop powers of The Third Eye, Spiritual Healing, Clairvoyance, Telekinesis and Psychokinesis.

Sincerely,

Anxious not to be thought to be encouraging the evils of gambling, a number of postal workers objected to handling premium bonds when they were first introduced.

Inside knowledge

Losing a betting slip and being unable to claim your winnings is always a problem for a punter. Even more so if you happen to be in the nick at the time!

So the punter who wrote to his bookie in mid-1978 clearly had a minor difficulty to sort out – particularly as he wasn't due to be released for another seven years.

He wrote, 'Dear Sir, I placed a bet with you in one of your offices on Thursday, 1 June. I'm sorry to say my copy is lost in prison, where I'm serving a long sentence. I have been sending out bets by the "back door" over the past sixteen months under *noms de plume*.

'As you will know, I'm breaking prison rules and security, and any leak that I have corresponded with you could cause serious trouble, so I cannot give you my name and address.

'I have been in prison since 1968 and I'm not due to be released until 1985, so there is no way at present that I could go to your office to fill in a claims form for my winnings.

'Sir, I would be very grateful if you could let the person whose name and address I will supply, act on my behalf to receive any winnings if you decide I should receive them.'

A little bird later told me that he was paid.

An engaging bet

Alec Stewart was a little reluctant to ask his girlfriend to marry him, and she couldn't understand why – until he confessed that he would lose a substantial bet on the day they became engaged.

In fact it cost him £1,500!

For racehorse-trainer Stewart was in the bet with fellow trainer Jamie Toller, assistant trainer Chris Thomson Jones, and Teddie Beckett of the British Bloodstock Agency. The stake was that the first of the four of them to become engaged should buy the others dinner in the restaurant of their choice.

They chose Le Pavillon on the Champs Elysées in Paris – or rather, that's where he took them. They'd first asked for a restaurant in New York!

According to Beckett, 'The restaurant was extremely expensive. We had Roederer Cristal champagne followed by Château Montrachet and all washed down with a 1930 Armagnac.'

Still, when he wed Katherine Domvile in 1986, Stewart confessed the expense was worthwhile!

Jimmy peters out

Lifelong punter Jimmy Peters was a regular visitor to a Cardiff betting shop.

So when sixty-year-old Jimmy sadly passed away in September 1985, his bookie, John Lovell, allowed the wake to take place in his betting shop!

Said Mr Lovell, 'It is the way he would have wanted to go – he spent most of his life in betting shops.'

Bookies conned

It isn't too often that the punters manage to pull the wool over the eyes of the bookies.

But in 1898, a still unknown group of con-men managed it in spectacular style – by inventing a race meeting, and its results!

The editor of the *Sportsman*, one of the most respected publications of the day, was asked by a man calling himself Mr Martin to publish the card for the Trodmore Hunt meeting of 1 August, which he duly did.

Many London bookies accepted bets on the various races and sat back to await the results which would appear in the next day's paper.

When the results came out, the bookies began to find an astonishing number of large winning bets on a horse called Reaper. Many of them shrugged and paid out immediately. Others, more suspicious, noticed that the results hadn't appeared in the *Sporting Life* and began to make enquiries. Maps were consulted, memories searched, but no trace could be found of Trodmore – nor of the man who asked the editor of the *Sportsman* to publish the card.

Of course, Trodmore had never existed, and embarrassed bookies were left with red faces and lighter pockets.

Heads you win

Punters often try to pick the brains of as many people as possible in their quest for winners – but few go to the extremes reported from Kuala Lumpur, Malaysia in 1986 when police hunting murderers, who had killed a man and stolen his brain, said they believed the crime had been committed to help bring the perpetrators luck in Malaysia's weekly lottery!

Mohamed Kassim Ismail, thirty-two, was discovered sitting upright in front of a temple with a deep head wound – and no brain. His money and watch were untouched.

Gilbert owns up

Gilbert Claughton of Cambridge paid William Hill 7½p for a football bet in October, 1980.

Nothing strange about that, you might think – except that he originally struck the bet on 8 November 1958 – twenty-two years earlier.

'The reason for the delay was that the bill got lodged inside an old football annual and I forgot all about it until an advert for Hill's in the *Daily Mirror* all those years later jogged my memory!'

Bolton bets

Contemporary reports tell of the odd wagering which went on in the mid-nineteenth century at the Halshaw Wakes held near Bolton where, apparently, people would bet on the ability of other people to eat scalding porridge with their fingers, to strip the wicks from a pound of candles with their teeth, and to eat eight pounds of treacle in twenty minutes!

Webbed winners

Associated Press reported a tragic tale in August 1983.

Five Filipino children had died of poisonous spider bites within a week in an area in which betting on spider fights had become a fad amongst school children.

Police at Digos, 650 miles south of Manila, said that they did not know which species of spider was involved.

Not to be sneezed at!

In 1977 I received a letter from a senior citizen who claimed to be able to infect people with a cold by talking to them for ten minutes.

Bill Davies from Caerphilly, Glamorgan, wrote, 'What odds will you give me against my producing a common cold within five to seven days under normal, everyday conditions, in three people selected by you or your doctor?

'I shall not subject them to any form of inducement other than being allowed ten minutes' talk with them. But they will not have had a cold within six weeks before the test. I have no medical qualifications – or any qualifications.'

I rang Bill and spoke to him; he wouldn't reveal his methods and we couldn't quite agree on the exact form a bet might take – but within forty-eight hours of speaking to him I was sneezing madly!

Money can't buy me ... a winner

He never got the chance to win money for punters, or to lose it for them, but Snaafi Dancer deserves a brief mention.

The world's priciest racehorse – he cost Sheikh Mohammed Al-Maktoum $10.2 million in 1982 – was retired in December 1985 without ever setting foot on a racecourse.

The only winner in the affair must have been Robert Sangster, who was outbid for Snaafi at the Keeneland Sales in Kentucky when the colt was a yearling.

Poor Snaafi also proved something of a failure at stud, too, enjoying his work but not managing consistently to produce the goods. Perhaps he'll improve with practice ...!

They're off!

A group of friends were in a pub in Ipswich prior to a local Sunday League match, discussing the financial plight of their team, Sorrel FC.

Player's wife Jan Sherwood suddenly offered to bet any takers that she would be prepared to do a streak during the match, with the proceeds of her winning bets to go to club funds!

There were plenty of people willing to bet her at even money, so shortly after half-time, the 300 spectators, the players, referee and linesmen were all stunned as Jan peeled off and raced across the pitch – to the absolute consternation of her twenty-eight-year-old husband Dave, who was playing in the game at the time!

> *Then there was the optimistic gambler who went to the races saying, 'I hope I break even this afternoon – I could do with the money!'*

Winner on a loser?

The mythical searches for the Holy Grail, the secret of eternal life and the mystery of the alchemist's art are as nothing compared with the frantic cravings of the average punter to discover the perfect betting system.

That system doesn't exist – but in 1982 a Cornish gentleman, who called himself Mr Winner, decided that it did, and he'd found it.

What to do with it? thought Mr Winner. Why not blackmail the bookies? So he wrote to me – asking for half a million pounds, or he would unleash his system upon my company!

Wrote Mr Winner, 'I have always believed that there was a system that would work. During the holidays last year I came up with what I considered to be a foolproof system. I watched the results every day and every day my system worked and showed an average profit of £2,000 each week.

'At present I am the only person who knows it. I thought about selling . . .

'When I realized the full potential of it, I decided to offer it to you thinking that you would want to buy it so that you could take out a world copyright on it. This would mean that I could not sell it to any other punters.

'My price for this system is £500,000.

'I obviously do not expect you to send a cheque for £500,000 through the post. When you have made your decision please send your reply to the address shown on my SAE.

'If you do not pay I promise that I will not only use it myself but I will tell it to a few mates and move around the country, and win that money within five years.'

I wrote to Mr Winner inviting him to try his system out in our shops. Shortly after he rang to tell me, 'Last week we 'ad £560, all right?'

Then he wrote, 'I did as you suggested. In the week ending 17.4.82 my total profit – excluding petrol – was £875.50. As you can see I am very serious about this matter of getting my deserved £500,000.'

Declaring he would now think about advertising the system, Mr Winner continued, 'If your bosses are daft enough to say no without even seeing me face to face, then say so as it will save me wondering whether to order my

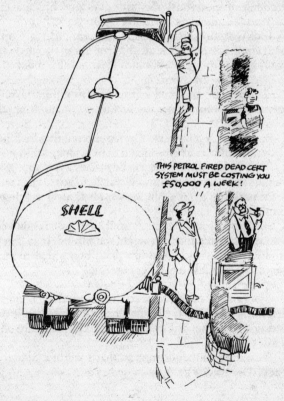

THIS PETROL FIRED DEAD CERT SYSTEM MUST BE COSTING YOU £50,000 A WEEK!

SHELL

new Lotus now, as there is a twenty-week waiting list, or leave it until the money comes pouring in from my advert.

'Do not forget that it is cheaper for you to pay me for my system than to be made bankrupt.'

And with that he was gone – never to be heard of again – and for all I know he may now be living it up on a tropical paradise island with enough money to burn. Then again, he may not!

Good old days?

A couple of apocryphal tales from days gone by.

At a chase meeting in the West Country before the First World War two army officers invested their all with a bookie on the final race of the day. As their fancy came bounding to the last a distance clear, so they noticed the bookie rapidly disappearing.

Giving chase they collared him outside the course and 'persuaded' him none too gently to hand over their winnings.

Returning to the course they discovered that their horse had tumbled over at the last and been beaten! . . .

. . . At a Haydock Park meeting many years ago, a long run of losing favourites looked certain to come to an end in a race where a 'good thing', especially laid out for the occasion, was due to oblige.

Digging deep, punters plunged their last resources on the animal, which consequently started red-hot favourite. In a close finish it looked like the favourite had won, but the name of a 20/1 shot went up in the frame as first past the post.

Disgruntled backers rushed to argue with the judge. Even the clerk of the course had (illegally) backed the favourite, and he said to the judge, 'That was a bit close, wasn't it?'

'Yes,' replied the judge, 'and that's the first winner I've backed for weeks!'

By royal appointment

Edward III was the first monarch to prohibit gambling, 'to protect manly sports and the military arts' which were being neglected by the wagering mad masses.

How successful he was can be gathered from the fact that Henry VIII had to repeat the performance, pronouncing gaming houses unlawful because they distracted young men from archery and military preparation – in other words, if the French had invaded he'd have had to ask them to hold on while he rounded up his army from the local betting shops!

Denis' disaster

On Cheltenham Gold Cup Day, 1985, the then shadow sports minister, Denis Howell, pulled off a feat most punters can only dream of by picking three winners with his three selections.

However, he wasn't too happy about it.

For, even as he was about to set out for Cheltenham and the day's racing, Labour leader Neil Kinnock sent him a message saying that he was needed in the House to put the Opposition case on soccer violence.

Howell produced a most aggressive speech, and fellow MPs assumed it was because he was peeved at missing the day's racing. When they enquired he confirmed that that was the case – but added that he had been even more aggrieved by not having had the time to get his bets on his three winners.

Patient punter

I had to look twice – and yet again – at the letter from a patient in a Liverpool hospital asking for a Grand National bet.

The letter arrived a couple of weeks before the big race, and with it was a cheque for £220 which was, explained the would-be punter, the stake money for the bet. He would ring us on the day of the race and tell us which horse he wished to back.

But the extraordinary thing was that the cheque enclosed was made out to William Hill Ltd. – and issued by the Department of Health and Social Security!

Just how the patient had managed to persuade them to make out a cheque to a bookie for a bet he hadn't even placed, really does make me wonder!

> *For the last three years William Hill have been official bookmakers to the World Black Pudding Championships.*

Betting bite

Snack eaters everywhere should be grateful to devoted gambler John Montagu – for without him they might not have one of their favourite forms of food to this day.

Montagu, born in 1718, was an inveterate card player. One day, whilst he was involved in a particularly important hand of cards for a great deal of money, he felt hungry. Rather than interrupt the hand, he called for some food to be placed between two slices of bread and brought to him. The new eating idea was a sensation and rapidly caught on, becoming known after its inventor, Montagu – who was also the fourth Earl of Sandwich!

She's the greatest

Punters found a new heroine to look up to in February 1986 when thirty-two-year-old Evelyn Adams of New Jersey won over a million dollars – for the second time in the space of four months.

In October 1985, Evelyn landed $3.9 million (£2.76 million) in the New Jersey Lotto lottery in which punters select six numbers to match with those drawn out by lottery officials.

She wasn't satisfied with just that, though. She had been spending $25 a week on lottery tickets, which she increased to $100. A 'small' win of $500 in an instant lottery gave notice that she was set to strike again – which she did in February 1986, winning $1.4 million (just short of £1 million).

That satisfied her. Her friends were getting jealous, she said, 'So I'm going to quit playing and give everyone else a chance.'

● The world's biggest single gambling loss (at least, reported loss) was by the anonymous Italian industrialist who left £800,000 behind in Monte Carlo in a five-hour roulette session in 1974.

Dying for a winner

As a man in a bingo hall slumped to the ground dying from a heart attack, all the 500 players wanted to do was get on with their game!

It happened in Reading, Berkshire in December 1985.

A nurse attempted to save the forty-two-year-old man by giving him the kiss of life and a chest massage as the sound of bingo numbers continued.

Said an eye witness, 'It was obvious the man was dying, but all that the people cared about was winning – the game should have been stopped straightaway.'

Bingo hall manager John Fordham thought that chaos would have ensued had he called the game off. 'I honestly think we did the best thing possible in the circumstances,' he was quoted as saying.

This was far from the first occasion that death and gambling had been seen together.

In the nineteenth century at White's, a London gentlemen's club famous for gambling, it was said that a man who collapsed outside outside the club's bow window was refused medical attention – because it might prejudice members' bets as to whether he lived or died!

On another occasion at the club, £1,000 was apparently wagered that a man could live for twelve hours under water. A 'low fellow' was hired, sunk in a boat – and the bet lost.

Cleo's gem
of a bet

Cleopatra, so I am reliably informed, took Mark Antony well and truly to the cleaners one night in around 1 BC when they were lying around idly carousing.

The great Egyptian beauty wagered that she could drink the Roman equivalent of about a quarter of a million pounds' worth of wine without getting up from her place.

Mark must have over-imbibed: he accepted the bet. Whereupon the clever Cleo dropped two or three ultra valuable pearls into her goblet of wine – and drank the lot.

Game, bet and match to Cleo.

An American sheriff was sacked from his job after a mouse he'd backed in a race failed to win – and he ate it!

Street's a grand programme

Loyalty to one of TV's longest running and most popular serials, *Coronation Street*, persuaded arts programme presenter Melvyn Bragg to enter into a £1,000 bet.

Bragg put his cash on the line in April 1985, when former Coronation Street scriptwriter Esther Rose predicted the show would be taken off the air after its twenty-fifth anniversary in November 1985.

Appearing on the breakfast show *TV*-am, Bragg wrote out a cheque for £1,000, his stake that the Street would live on. 'I invited Esther to accept my bet. She said she would but didn't offer a cheque.'

Bragg also said that if he lost the bet he'd like Esther to donate his stake to the Save The Children Fund.

Esther hit back, 'Of course I accepted his bet ... and I'm sure I'll win.'

Of course, the Street is still going strong, but sadly Esther died before the bet had run its course.

... The Street's popularity also provided a West Midlands bookie with a regular flow of bets – he offered odds against the number of times the word 'flaming' was used in any one episode!

The odds ranged from 10/1 for no 'flamings' to 66/1 for ten! ...

... I upset the Street's Public Relations boss, Norman Frisby, when I made the programme's fierce rival, *EastEnders*, favourite to win the battle for viewers at Christmas, 1985.

Mr Frisby came on the phone to me complaining that we were misleading punters because the *EastEnders* viewing figures were unfairly calculated on weekday viewers plus people watching the Sunday omnibus edition.

He was not placated when I told him we could only bet

on the official figures produced by the British Audience Research Bureau, which always included the omnibus . . .

. . . Former Street actor Fred Feast, who played barman Fred Gee, tells how he backed a long-priced winner once. 'Sometimes while shooting behind the bar, Julie Goodyear (Bet Lynch) jokingly said, "Fred, don't touch me." And on one occasion I just happened to notice that a horse called Don't Touch was running that afternoon – Julie doesn't normally have a bet but she put £1 on, and it went in at 25/1.'

> **Twenty-four-year-old Irishman Eric Daly won $6.3 million in the California State Lottery. He handed his good luck charm, a rhinestone shamrock, to a stranger standing next to him – twenty-five-year-old Samuel Heath – who promptly won $1 million with the next spin of the lottery wheel.**

Tricky for Paul

On just one occasion has Paul Daniels employed his magical talents to land a gamble. In the early, less successful days of his career he was on board a cross-channel ferry, and had no money after his bags had been stolen. He joined in a game of cards with three Frenchmen.

'I hadn't eaten for three days. Using sleight of hand I won the first hand and bought myself some sandwiches! I know it was a bit naughty, but honestly, I was desperate.'

But there was one trick, later, that proved to be beyond even him – getting his three-year-old filly, That's Magic, to win. Paul, who says 'I am not a heavy gambler but I do like a flutter', sponsored the Paul Daniels Magic Handicap at Redcar and entered That's Magic, who could only finish fifteenth out of the eighteen starters.

A grand bet –
fifty times over!

The biggest single betting-shop cash bet ever reported occurred on Derby Day, 1985, when a punter strolled into a Park Lane shop situated midway between the Hilton and the Dorchester Hotels, and told staff, 'I'd like to make a little bet on Shadeed, please.'

He then pulled bundles and bundles of £50 notes out of his pocket and calmly handed them over – staking £50,000 in all!

At the odds he took, 5/2, the punter stood to make a profit of £125,000, but to the relief of the manager the horse was beaten.

Teeing up a
winner

Just as the 1983 British Open Golf Tournament was about to begin, a client in a Southport betting shop enquired about a price for Scottish golfer Sam Torrance to win the event.

'66/1,' said the manager.

'He's got no chance – should be 166/1,' came a call from the back of the office.

The surprised punter and manager turned as the owner of the voice came up to the counter and told the punter to keep his money for Torrance to win the Tournament, but to back him instead to finish as Top British Player.

'What do you know about it?' asked the punter.

'I'm Sam Torrance,' said the golf pundit.

◇ 30 ◇

Dead cert

Racing-form expert Marten Julian was surprised by the contents of a recently deceased friend's will.

For Julian was left £1,000 by journalist and radio presenter Derek Jewell, who died in November 1985, 'with the request that he uses the sum to be wagered on four horses of his choice.' Jewell's will went on to stipulate that 90% of any winnings must be donated to the Injured Jockeys Fund and the remaining 10% be used by Julian to buy racing books.

Commented Julian, 'Derek loved multiple bets and so it will be very much in the spirit of the legacy that the bets should be made to win huge amounts.' Julian later told me he'd made £300 profit on the stake.

> *Former soccer star Stan Bowles loved a bet. In fact, he told a tale of joining Gamblers Anonymous to try to beat the bug – but he ended up betting on how long he would stay with the therapy group!*

Royal flush

After she died in April 1986, it was reported in the *Daily Telegraph* that the Duchess of Windsor was a skilled poker player and that her ability 'enabled her usefully to supplement her slender income' when she and her first husband lived in Peking in the 1920s.

Webber's winner

Julian Lloyd Webber and Andrew Lloyd Webber are brothers who have been very successful in the music business. They are both supporters of Orient Football Club.

However, while Julian remained a fanatical supporter, Andrew's loyalty began to wane.

So, one season, when Orient needed a point to avoid relegation with one match to play, Andrew bet Julian they wouldn't get it – and staked writing Julian some music on the outcome of the wager.

Orient won the point; Julian won the music. It turned into the hit album *Variations* and went gold.

Appropriately enough, Julian presented the gold disc for the record to the Orient chairman in the centre circle just before the start of a home match. They lost the match!

Lottery luck –
or lack of!

Fifty-two-year-old housewife Doris Barnett was a millionaire – for three seconds.

The Los Angeles lady saw her ball jump into the top prize slot worth some $3,000,000 (£2,000,000) in the Californian State Lottery in January 1986. To win that amount it had to stay there for five seconds – but it dropped out two seconds early, and Doris was left with a consolation prize of about $11,000 (£7,000) . . .

. . . When Egyptian Asfor Beg died he followed an old custom of being buried with all his worldly goods, including a raffle ticket. Some time later his widow went to the local coroner and persuaded him to allow her to exhume the body to reclaim the lottery ticket – which won her £10,000.

With part of the money she bought him a new grave-stone...

...The garage customer in Akrolimni, northern Greece, couldn't pay his petrol bill, so he gave attendant Constantine Popodis, aged twenty-eight, £4 of lottery tickets – with which he won £180,000...

...Jim Cohoon of Toronto won the equivalent of £350,000 in a lottery in early 1985. Three months later he had given it all away, was on the dole and living in a hostel. He said, 'I've no regrets – but it might have been different if I hadn't been drinking so much!'...

... Delighted winners on the California State Lottery have been brought down to earth when they've learnt that their winnings have been confiscated to pay off their state government debts. By the end of 1985 over $100,000 (£77,000) in winnings had been used to pay off parking tickets, income tax debts and child support. Winning names are run through a computer full of debt details. Elliott Dixon won $1,000 in the lottery – but it all went in back payments to his estranged wife!

Hyde seeks ghost winners

English actor Wilfrid Hyde White hasn't had the ghost of a chance of backing a winner for over fifty years!

For the veteran actor has a story of how, in 1935, he went to Ascot racecourse before the Royal Meeting for a stroll around, only to experience the apparition of a meeting taking place. Hyde White says that a voice began to announce runners and riders – a system then not even invented – and that while he and a friend listened the names of the winners of all the races on the card were announced.

Hyde White, a keen follower of the turf, didn't recognize the names of any of the phantom runners, and is still waiting to this day for the meeting to take place!

In a matter of months during 1982, thirty-three-year-old Gary Llewellyn of Des Moines, Iowa, lost fifteen million dollars in Las Vegas casinos, which he had 'acquired' by dubious means from his father's bank. He was brought to trial and found insane.

Longest odds ever?

In 1967, William Hill laid an ante-post bet at the longest odds ever. How long? Well, seventy-five yards, to be precise!

For their client took ante-post prices on eight selections in the Cesarewitch, seven on the Cambridgeshire, four in the Arc de Triomphe and five in the November Handicap, and wanted them coupled up in 1,120 accumulators, 638 trebles and 26 doubles for an outlay of over £5,000.

By the time the client's bet had been converted to an ante-post voucher it was 225 feet long – all of which was crammed into an envelope and sent off to him. He didn't back one winner!

Dear Sir:

I am a member of the Central Florida Nuclear Freeze Campaign and I need your help. We would like your professional opinion on the odds that there will be a nuclear war within the next 3 years. (Before 11 May, 1986).

We define "a nuclear war" as any war, combat or action between two or more parties in which one or more nuclear weapons is used resulting in 100,000 casualties or more.

Enclosed is a check for $5.00 to help cover your postage and handling expenses.

Thank you,

Harry's bet in a million

Factory worker Harry Ward, who left Britain for America in 1958, never forgot the friend who bet him £100 that he couldn't make money out of selling cars.

So when he became a millionaire – heading a thriving car sales chain, owning a Rolls Royce Silver Cloud and a fourteen-room ranch-house – he came looking for the cash.

Said Harry, who also became Mayor of Westworth, Texas, 'I collected my £100 on a business trip to Britain.'

Sam's no foxy punter

Page three girl Samantha Fox, Britain's favourite pin-up, revealed that despite her popularity with punters – she's twice been favourite to win the Page Three Girl of the Year title and duly did so – she knows nothing about betting.

I met Sam when she opened a brand new betting shop in West London in early 1986; we offered her a free £100 bet on behalf of the charity of her choice. She opted for Help The Aged, but when I asked her what she wanted to back she said, 'I don't know, I've never backed a horse before, what do you suggest?'

Between us we picked out a namesake – Sam's Neighbour – which ran badly enough to suggest that a new career as a professional gambler is not likely for Sam! Still, the charity benefited by a hundred quid, anyway, when we donated her stake money on her behalf.

Beau's bag

Beau Brummel, whose sense of fashion means that he is still famous today, once enjoyed an afternoon's shooting.

Confident of his abilities with a gun, Beau wagered a substantial sum with his host that he would take the heaviest bag of anyone on the shoot.

The host accepted, and was doing rather better than Beau as the day drew to a close.

Nothing if not resourceful, Beau took rather a desperate measure to ensure that his bag was indeed heavier than anyone else's – he shot the host's pointer bitch!

A funny thing happened at the bookies (1)

A keen gambling bus conductor I know in Harrow, Middlesex, was in the betting shop on the morning of his wedding day with just fifty pence in his pocket and no ring to slip on his beloved's finger – he'd lost all his money at Wembley Dogs the night before. He staked the fifty pence on a forecast bet at the morning greyhound meeting – and won enough to buy a modest ring. Yet he still had to be forced out of the shop to go and *buy* it – he said he was on a winning streak and ought to gamble what he'd won! . . .

. . . The old boy in the Hull betting shop collapsed shortly before the last race. Concerned staff and customers called an ambulance. A couple of days later he returned and the clientele were stunned when he collapsed again. Once again the ambulance took him off to hospital. When he came back the next week and collapsed again suspicions were aroused, and the man confessed he was pulling the stunt to get free 'bed and breakfast'. . . .

... A punter in a Lancashire shop collapsed, genuinely suffering from a heart attack. The ambulance arrived, he was put gently on a stretcher and carried out. As he reached the door he called out in a touch of panic – 'I haven't put me bet on yet!'. ...

... The manager of a betting shop owned by one of the large chains was dismissed when, returning to the shop after a lunchtime tipple, he proceeded to bombard his staff and customers with cream cakes! His appeal for unfair dismissal was rejected.

On the level

The bookie decided he really couldn't offer a price when two steam roller enthusiasts asked him to lay odds on the chances of their being run over by one of the chugging machines!

For the punters were a father and son who attended as many steam rallies as possible and decided it would be in their interest to cover themselves against the worst happening.

They were turned down flat!

Golé!

Staff at the betting shop in Denny, Stirling, Scotland, were surprised to receive a picture postcard from Spain in 1982.

On the back was the message, 'Thanking your organization for the financial aid in the last football fixed odds season. Travelling through Spain watching World Cup soccer – f***ing great. A. Client'!

Little Johnny had a gambling problem. His worried father and teacher got together to discuss it.

'What he really needs is the shock of losing a large amount of pocket money – that will bring him to his senses,' said the teacher. 'I'll wait for the right opportunity and try to arrange it.'

Next day, little Johnny was, as usual, persuading classmates to bet with him in the playground. His teacher heard him whispering to a pal, 'I bet I know what colour knickers Miss is wearing.'

Teacher pounced. 'Ah, Johnny, so you think you know what colour knickers I'm wearing? I bet you five pounds you don't.'

'Please, Miss, they're red, Miss.'

Teacher lifted her dress to reveal blue underwear. 'Now hand over the five pounds, Johnny, and let that be a lesson – it doesn't pay to gamble.'

Triumphantly Teacher rang Johnny's father. 'It worked, I think we've finally cured him. I overheard him telling a classmate he knew what colour knickers I had on, so I bet him he didn't and won five pounds from him – that should be the end of his gambling.'

Replied the father, gloomily, 'I don't think so – before he left for school this morning Johnny bet me £10 he could get you to lift up your dress in the playground and show off your knickers!'

Cram's hat trick

British runner Steve Cram amused reporters after he had just won a silver medal in the Olympic Games 1500 metres in 1984 by turning up to the press reception wearing a peaked cap surmounted by a pair of clapping hands, which he manipulated with a string!

Cram had wagered with the ITN TV camera crew that he would wear the hat, whether he won or lost.

A lice idea

A Devon doctor anticipates a new boom sport for punters to bet on – woodlice racing!

Dr Terence Glanvill of Honiton has invented a ten-race track for woodlice and is convinced the new sport will 'take off in a big way'.

The doctor was reported as saying, 'They go even faster if you place a damp cloth on the track, and the thing with woodlice is that you can paint numbers on their backs to identify them.'

Aspiring to greatness

Jack Fuller might have had a drop or two, but he damned well knew what could or couldn't be seen from his drawing-room window, at home in Kent.

Yet another fellow in their London club on this night in the early nineteenth century was telling Jack that he couldn't possibly see the spire of Dallington Church from that room. 'Absolute rot,' said Jack, 'and to prove it, I'll wager 1,000 guineas that it can be seen.'

Returning home, Jack was not a little concerned to discover that no matter what position he adopted the spire of Dallington Church just couldn't be glimpsed from his window – other buildings were getting in the way.

Inspiration struck! Jack donated enough to the church to enable them to heighten the spire by forty feet – it might have cost more than the original stake, but at least he won the bet!

Stung into action

Most people talk to rock superstar Sting about music. However, when I interviewed Sting he told me how he stumbled into the world of racing. 'I had six Irish builders in my house and we got talking. "Sting," they said, "what you need with all your money is a whole string of racehorses."'

When he showed interest they revealed that it just so happened 'one of them had a horse called Sweetcal, and Jerry Reilly and I went into partnership. What they hadn't told me was that Sweetcal also pulled a milk cart! She wasn't very good.'

Not very good, perhaps, but still good enough to land a couple of nice wins for Sting, alias Gordon Sumner, at odds of 33/1 and 14/1.

Sting has also owned several other horses, notably the useful Sandalay. Appropriately enough, his racing colours are black and yellow.

'I always back my horses because I think it's in good faith to do so. I always back them to win a reasonable amount of money, and do fairly well out of it. But I don't gamble outside of racing – I'm not a gambling man.'

Nor is he ever likely to ride one of his own horses to victory, despite being a keen rider – he's too heavy for a jockey. He also revealed to me that 'The first time I ever rode a horse was in Egypt when we were riding round the Pyramids on Arabian stallions. It was just like riding a motorbike without handles – an unforgettable experience.'

Babe's Bentley bet

In 1931, eccentric millionaire Woolf 'Babe' Barnato bet a friend leaving Monte Carlo on the famous Blue Train that he would be back in England in his Bentley Silent Speed Six before the express could even reach Calais.

Barnato, an enthusiastic gambler, won the bet – £100 – but was fined £160 for holding an unauthorized contest.

The car was valued at £200,000 when it came up for auction in 1984. Artist Terence Cuneo has immortalized the wager in a famous painting of the race.

TV's Sergeant Bilko was notorious for getting the better of his army colleagues, often over dubious gambles. But ironically, when the actor who played Bilko, Phil Silvers, died in 1985 he was reportedly penniless after losing it all at cards.

Bet and breakfast

The only inn in the country with its own betting shop was the twenty-four-bedroom Hyperion in Fairford, Gloucester. It was run by hotelier/bookmaker Michael Gannon until he sold it in mid-1984.

Another unusually located betting shop was the one which operated from a former police cell in 1963.

Mel's funny sideline

Comedian and comic writer Mel Smith is a proficient punter. It is the bookies' good fortune that Smith is kept fully occupied with his show business activities these days; for when he was in a position to concentrate on winning money, he proved most adept at it.

Mel, whose dad was a bookie, and a friend became professional gamblers for six months after leaving Oxford University. 'There are so many unknown factors in deciding which horse is going to win a race,' he was quoted as saying. 'You can only amass a certain number of them on your side at one time. 'But we worked hard at it. Every day there was racing we went. Off the track we spent all our waking hours reading the form books, poring over the results.'

Nowadays Mel bets mainly for fun – on anything from the total of a restaurant bill to his hand in a poker game.

● Mel's gambling experiences paid off when he wrote and starred in a play, *The Gambler*, which enjoyed a successful run in 1986. Before the performance Mel would often step out and offer to bet the audience double or quits on the price of their tickets!

Bailing out the bookie

Pensioner John Hunt sent his pal off with a tenner to put on a horse for him, so he was expecting a return of £25 when the horse won. But his pal came back and confessed, 'I lent your money to the bookie and didn't have anything left for the bet!' For thirty-three-year-old John Sebine had come to the rescue of his local bookie in Harehills, Leeds, who had run out of cash and couldn't pay his customers.

John lent them every penny he had on him – £70 – then suddenly realized he hadn't any cash left for his mate's bet on Something Special. And, of course, it romped home at 6/4.

Said pensioner John, 'When he told me what he'd done I called him every name under the sun, but now I can see the funny side. I bet we're the only men in the country to have lent the bookies money.'

Refuse collector John Sebine said ruefully, 'There was a big queue of winning punters and an empty till. I felt sorry for them and lent them all my cash, including John's £10.'

What a goal, goal!

When did two footballers score the same goal?

The answer is in the 1979 Cup Final when both Brian Talbot and Alan Sunderland seemed to hit the ball at exactly the same moment for Arsenal's first goal.

Observers, fans, players and officials were all baffled. Talbot was eventually credited with the goal, but bookies decided that it was impossible to split them and paid out on both to punters who had bet on who would score the first goal.

Calling the tune

In the 1950s, bandleader Maurice Winnick used to present the TV programme *What's My Line*. He was also a keen punter and once asked a bookmaker for a bet of £400. The bookie said he would only accept £40.

Winnick asked him whether he knew who he was. When the bookie said 'Yes', Winnick asked whether the bookie would like to appear on the programme. He said he would.

'You'll do well,' said Winnick. 'Nobody will ever guess you are a bloody bookmaker.'

Dear Sir,

Would you lay me odds concerning U.F.O's becoming a proven fact and the origin of some of them recognised by at least two major-powers, (America, Russia, Great-Britain, France, Canada, Australia) within ten years.

I believe them to be controlled by intelligent beings and feel this may be proved by at least two of the countries mentioned. Also where some of them come from established as fact.

Yours sincerely

I'LL HAVE THE SAME AS HIM, PLEASE. WHOSE BATS ARE THEY?

Batty bet

Piers Sherlock put regulars at his local pub into a flap – by eating a bat to win a bet!

Piers, twenty-one at the time, accidentally killed the bat with his car on the way to The Crown pub at Weston, Northants. He took it into the bar with him – whereupon twenty of the drinkers put up £35 that he wouldn't eat the bat.

'It seemed like a good idea,' said Piers, who promptly downed the creature, with the help of a pint of bitter. 'I spent the winnings on a celebration,' he added.

Joe on cue

After Joe Johnson landed the biggest upset ever in the snooker world by winning the Embassy World Championship in May 1986, his manager, John Cocker, told how the man who had begun the event a 150/1 no-hoper came by his cue.

Cocker said that Johnson won it twenty years ago after making a bet with a one-armed snooker player! 'By the end of that session the lad owed Joe 7/6^d (37½p). He couldn't pay and said Joe may as well have his cue. Joe's used it ever since.'

Erik stubs out rivals

Danish motor-cyclist Erik Gundersen clinched the 1984 World Speedway Championship, helped by a £1,000 bet that he couldn't give up smoking.

The champion revealed, 'I used to smoke twenty a day, but I was getting out of breath and wouldn't have been fit enough to become champion.

'Then, earlier in the season, Suzanne, the girlfriend of Hans Nielsen (a rival rider), saw me puffing away at a cigarette between heats.

'She told me I was crazy and bet me £1,000 I couldn't go a year without smoking. But I haven't touched a cigarette since and now I'm looking forward to collecting the cash.'

Q. **What do you get when you add a pony to a monkey?**
A. £525. (Pony is gambling slang for £25, monkey means £500.)

Red bet gone
for a Burton

Superstar actor Richard Burton was buried dressed in red. This was probably the first time that anyone had ever won a bet from beyond the grave.

Fifty-eight-year-old Burton had once bet fellow actors Peter O'Toole and Stanley Baker that they would never manage to catch him not wearing something in red – the national colour, of course, of his beloved country, Wales.

Every day for many years, Burton wore red to maintain the bet, and when he was buried in August 1984 he wore a red jacket, red trousers, red polo neck jumper and red socks. His brother, Verdun Jenkins, told reporters, 'I can see him up there now, laughing his head off after so decisively winning the bet.'

Murphy's missing

Organizing a draw on Friday the 13th seemed a bad idea from the start, and it proved to be just that in Ireland in September 1985 when the ticket winning a £500 pony was drawn out with one word on it – Murphy.

There are 10,000 families of that name in the Irish Republic.

Weeks later the organizers were still trying to trace the winner – and were being inundated with claims from Murphys of all types!

They'd even had a claim from a man whose name wasn't Murphy, but who claimed that if ever he buys a raffle ticket when he has a few drinks in him, he signs his name as Murphy!

Punter all at sea

Erick John Peters is a confident man, which is just as well, for in 1982 he was preparing to cross the Atlantic – in a 5′10½″ barrel!

Mr Peters, of Sussex, wanted his bookies to bet on whether he could do it. They declined, politely suggesting that this was a venture which might end in disaster.

I wonder if he made it?

Howzat!

Larger than life Australian test bowler Dennis Lillee hit the headlines when he backed England to win a Test Match.

What's wrong with that?

Nothing much, except that the Test Match was against Australia – and Lillee was playing!

At the time, England seemed down and out, and were being quoted on the ground at the fantastic odds of 500/1. Lillee self-confessedly invested a tenner which he turned into £5,000 – and then walked into a storm of Aussie criticism! . . .

. . . One of the greatest cricketers of all time was Sir Gary Sobers – and a bet inspired him to one of the most memorable feats ever recorded on a cricket ground. Before going out to bat against Glamorgan on 31 August 1968, Sir Gary had backed three horses: Gipsy Bridge, Mycropolis and Jubilation. They all won – at odds of 10/1, 20/1 and 4/1 – and Sir Gary promptly went out to bat and hit six sixes in one over off poor Malcolm Nash! . . .

. . . One cricketer who didn't do quite so well out of a bet was Younis Ahmed, who was sacked from the Worcestershire side after being accused of placing a £100 wager.

The fact that the match on which he was accused of placing the bet, a John Player League match between Worcester and Leicester, was abandoned, was deemed to be irrelevant.

Ahmed was alleged to have placed the bet on his own side being beaten and was sacked for 'gross misconduct'.

The Irish priest was bequeathed a donkey by a departed parishioner.
Father Murphy soon discovered that the donkey was a very fast runner.
Thinking he might win some money for parish funds, he entered him in a race. The donkey came third and the local paper ran a story headlined 'Father Murphy's Ass Shows'.
The archbishop saw the paper and was not amused, but by then the priest had entered the donkey for another race, which it won. Whereupon the paper shouted, 'Father Murphy's Ass Out In Front'.
The archbishop immediately banned the priest from running the horse in any more races. Said the paper, 'Archbishop Scratches Father Murphy's Ass'.
Sell the donkey, or get rid of it, the archbishop told Father Murphy, who reluctantly gave it to a nun he knew.
'Father Murphy Gives His Ass To Sister Agatha' trumpeted the paper.
The archbishop was by now being driven to distraction and demanded that Sister Agatha dispose of the donkey. She sold it for £10.
'Sister Agatha Sells Her Ass For £10' ran the newspaper headline.
The archbishop went out and got drunk!

Gambling with 'Er Indoors

Asian folk tales of long ago tell stories of men who gambled using their wives, sisters and daughters as stakes.

Occasionally, if there was no female around to wager with, they would risk various limbs from their bodies!

Trooping along for a bet

The pomp and pageantry of the Trooping the Colour ceremony is famed throughout the world. But there are people who watch the ceremony not for its splendour but in the hope that various members of the Household Cavalry will fall off their horses! There is a brisk betting market on the event. At a recent Trooping, much money was put on one adjutant not remaining on his steed.

The *Household Brigade* magazine later reported, 'But all punters were disappointed.'

Dear Sir or Madam,

You may find this letter a little bit strange, but I am writing to you with a request you may have had in the past or you may not. I only hope you don't send some men in white coats around for me, because I'd like you to arrange for me a wager. I'd like to place a £2 bet that Britain will have its coldest winter for 80 years and that within the next two years there will be a flood in Ethiopia I'd like you to get me as long odds as you can because if it comes off I'll donate eighty per cent of my winnings to Ethiopia. As I'm unemployed you'll appreciate the £2 has been hard to find but I'm just sitting here on a Wednesday afternoon twiddling my fingers and I thought I'd write to you. I don't know how long I'll be in this situation and a bet like this will give me a bit of interest, even if it's only in the weather forecasts. If you put the bet on and in the unlikely event it doesn't come off, I'll send another £2 to the Ethiopian funds without a wager.

Yours sincerely

Against all odds

Gerard Darroch of Scotland is nothing if not game.

He wrote to ask whether my company would offer odds against his winning the Glasgow Marathon in 1984 – giving the following guide to his chances, 'I am fifty-seven years old . . . I am on sick benefit with osteo-arthritis of the knee, and elsewhere I have a duodenal ulcer and a prolapsed disc . . . I have never run in a competitive race.'

Sadly, I couldn't take Mr Darroch's query seriously and declined to offer odds, but he was definitely serious, as he revealed in a further letter granting permission for his name to be used here, 'only if you sportingly acknowledge that you funked the challenge,' and suggesting that he might yet plan a tilt at the 1986 race!

Um heap bad bet!

In a desperate effort to improve Britain's summer weather in the damp August of 1985, a Red Indian bet that his sun-dance would send the temperature up to eighty degrees within two days.

Chief Shilo staked £25 at odds of 10/1 that his dance would reverse the trend which eventually earned August 1985 the title of the wettest month of all time; but the dance failed dismally, and it went on to rain, and rain, and rain!

Hills had been offering odds of 25/1 against it raining every single day of that month, and despite one punter taking a bet that the temperature would hit 107 during August, still it rained on – until Bank Holiday Monday, 26 August.

Dead loss

One of the most morbid requests for a bet came from a man in Enfield, London, who asked me what odds would be offered against his mother living for another five years. She was ninety-one at the time.

It was a sad story. He explained that he had had to give up work to look after her and was worried about his diminishing financial position.

He ended his letter with a strange paragraph. 'I have an account with Ladbrokes, but have not approached them as I thought your company the best for this type of offer'!

Virgin on the ridiculous!

Keith Morgan, who works for William Hill in their London headquarters, still laughs at the memory of the letters he received from a Cypriot businessman.

The man's daughter, remembers Keith, was about to be sent to England to become an au pair, and her father was a little concerned because he had heard certain stories about the rather loose morals of some of the younger element of English male society.

What he would like to know was what odds would the bookies be prepared to offer that his daughter would return to him in two years' time in the same untouched condition in which she was leaving him?

Keith and his colleagues spent a day or two considering if it were possible to set conditions for such a bet and how they might go about ascertaining whether it had been won or lost at the end of the specified period. But before he could draft a reply, he received another letter from the businessman.

The second letter regretted to inform the company that the bet must now be cancelled as his daughter wasn't coming to be an au pair after all – she was pregnant by a local romeo and would have to get married!

System in a spin

Even high technology computer know-how can't help you become 'the man who broke the bank at Monte Carlo', it seems.

A group of Californian physicists spent five years and $15,000 designing electronic brains which would predict the outcome of each spin of a roulette wheel.

They were made small enough to smuggle into a casino in the sole of a hollowed out shoe, and it was thought they would give their operator a 44% advantage over the house.

The computers were extremely sophisticated – designed to track the ball as it spun around the wheel, calculate the forces of friction and drag, adjust for tilt and change of speed, plot trajectories and predict where the ball would end up.

Electronic vibrators would tickle the underside of the gambler's foot, giving a signal as to which set of numbers to back.

The team tried out their scheme at the Horseshoe Club in Las Vegas. First indications were promising as the computer indicated 1, 13, 24 or 36, and 13 came up.

Then, disaster. The vibrators began to buzz at random and give the wrong signals. One player lifted his shoe up to his ear to try to sort out what was happening – and was immediately chased out of the casino.

Thomas Bass, a member of the team, concluded that interference from electronic surveillance cameras was to

blame for sending the computers haywire, and recalled how another US scientist, Claude Shannon of the Massachusetts Institute of Technology, had also once tried to beat the system with a computer plugged into his hearing aid. The result: 'Broken wires, gibbering beeps, shocks and electronic failures,' said Bass.

Now Bass and his colleagues have retired, hurt, to the drawing board, warning that at present no system other than pure luck exists which can help a punter beat the bank at roulette.

● The nearest thing to the 'perfect system' may have belonged to William Jaggens, a nineteenth-century French engineer alleged to have won one and a half million francs in a day and a half – before dying without revealing how he did it.

Little for Wood

Sixty-one-year-old grandmother Elizabeth Wood from Kent thought she had won £215,000 on the pools with Littlewoods in November 1985. But her stake had been pocketed by a crooked collector — who was later fined £50 for stealing her £4.32.

Mrs Wood received nothing.

Mike's losing streak

On 4 August 1975, twenty-four-year-old Michael Angelow was offered, and accepted, a £20 bet. Watched by 20,000 spectators and a television audience of millions, Michael, naked but for his shoes and socks, then ran on to the cricket pitch at Lords during the England versus Australia test match and leapt over the stumps.

The fifteen-stone ship's cook made his dash into history in ninety-degree heat and ran 500 yards before being escorted from the pitch.

He later commented, 'I was well and truly plastered,' and was relieved of his winnings by a local magistrate. An MCC spokesman said, 'It isn't cricket, but we were mildly amused.'

Nigel Dempster, gossip columnist of the *Daily Mail*, is married to Camilla, daughter of the eleventh Duke of Leeds. Says Dempster, 'She has lots of illustrious ancestors who owned vast tracts of England – she says the fourth Duke won their castle and 60,000 acres in a snail race.'

Oh, oh, seven

Sean 'James Bond' Connery and TV chat show host Michael Parkinson became involved in a strange wrangle over a wager, which apparently neither of them could really recall.

Connery was quoted as saying he would not appear on any Parkinson show because he was a 'welsher'.

'Parkinson owes me money,' claimed Connery, 'and I won't have anything to do with him until he pays up.'

Connery alleged that the pair had had a £10 bet on a football match involving Manchester United and that he had won.

Parkinson retaliated, 'I've got no intention of paying him the £10 I owe him until we meet face to face. He writes to me occasionally and reminds me about the money. The bet was actually over a friendly game between Leeds United and Celtic.'

In 1985 readers of the *Daily Mail* were presented with the hot news that the Queen Mother had given up betting. No longer did her private secretary, Sir Martin Gilliat, have to dash round the corner to the local bookies to place the royal wagers. However, following further investigation I can now put the record straight. The Queen Mother, who was honoured for her lifelong support for jump racing by the William Hill Golden Spur Award, doesn't bet at all, and never has. Her personal press officer, Major A. Griffin, informed me, 'I regret that Sir Martin was misquoted. Her Majesty does not bet and to the best of my knowledge never has done.' They do say she has her own private 'blower system' broadcasting daily racing information to her home, though!

No rasher bet!

Pig races are few and far between, but one well-documented example involved a side stake of £1,000.

In the nineteenth century, esteemed gentleman race-horse owner Dr Hutton had all his horses with trainer Harry Barnes of Ilsley, Yorkshire. Hutton was particularly proud of the training prowess of Barnes and was once heard to remark to two wealthy friends, 'I'll back that man to train anything.'

The friends, Mr Walter Long from Christ Church College, Oxford and Mr Lamont Rose of Brazenose were most interested. 'There's one thing I'll wager he can't do,' said Mr Long. 'Train a pig to jump hurdles!'

Dr Hutton did not back down and a £1,000 bet was struck – Mr Long and Mr Rose each putting up £500 of their own to match the stake. To win the bet for Dr Hutton, Barnes had to train eight porcine specimens to clear a course of eight flights of hurdles two feet six inches high.

Barnes got to work and devised a means of achieving this unheard-of feat. He first laid out the course of fixed hurdles, with others alongside to prevent the grunters from running out. He starved his animals during the day, then stood lads with food pails at the end of the course – and began to teach the pigs that it was a case of jump or starve!

After several weeks Barnes felt he was ready. The whole village turned out to watch.

The pigs, which had been kept away from food for a whole day, were lined up. Harry Barnes set off, jumping the hurdles himself, carrying a steaming food pail. At the same time the lads at the end of the course banged and rattled their own pails.

Sure enough, away went the pigs, snorting, stumbling, jumping, charging and grunting. To the cheers of the excited crowd, the whole field finally made it around the course, and with good grace Messrs Long and Rose paid over the £1,000 to a delighted Dr Hutton.

It is not recorded whether they got some of their own back by going off for a hearty meal of bacon and pigs' trotters.

The man who 'knew'

Self-styled psychic Jack Grant was a little concerned for the bookies when he discovered that they were accepting bets on the outcome of the Academy Awards, because he was sure he knew who was going to get two of the most important Oscars.

So, anxious to alert the bookmakers, he wrote from California to tell them who would win.

'I have heard of some bookmakers taking bets on the Academy Awards.

'I am psychic and have successfully predicted the winners of the Academy Awards since 1953. I do not ever know the winners to all the events, but make very few predictions. Doing so is the reason for my high success rate. I "know" by a feeling and so far have been 100% accurate concerning these awards.

'Here are the winners for this year (1984) in the categories of Best Actor and Best Actress: Best Actor, Robert Duvall; Best Actress, Meryl Streep.

'I hope this is of help to you.'

Well, it might have been had he been 100% right again – unfortunately, Meryl Streep was beaten by Shirley Mac-Laine. Jack had better polish up his crystal balls!

Henry VIII is said to have lost the bells of St Paul's in a dice game.

Punter's explosive revenge

Losing punters are seldom happy people – however, few of them attempt to blow up the racecourse where their ill fortune occurred!

In April 1985, at Beirut's Palace of Peace race track, the horses lined up for the start of the third race.

Suddenly, four of the most fancied horses fell, leaving a 91/1 long shot, Commodore, to romp home.

Hundreds of losing punters swarmed on to the track in protest, trampling over fences and tearing down the display board. After fifteen minutes of bedlam it was announced that the race was cancelled and all bets would be refunded.

The decision pleased the crowd, but enraged a man who had bet eleven dollars on Commodore. He threatened to blow up the track if he didn't get his winnings.

Police threw him out and order was restored.

Minutes later a rocket-propelled grenade fired by an unidentified gunner hit the track!

No one was injured, but the track was shut down.

Running out of luck

Twenty-seven-year-old Yugoslav policeman Sinisa Micic won £40,000 in a lottery in March 1986. He went to a bar at Smederevo, Belgrade to celebrate, ordered drinks all round, had a couple himself, took his leave, walked out of the bar – and was hit by a lorry and killed.

Dear Sir,

What odds will you give me that I can transmute gold into tin, in my mouth, before 1984, without blowing my head off?

Yours faithfully

Shanghaied

Following complaints in the *People's Daily* that lotteries were harming the public interest and corroding Chinese minds, authorities banned them in April 1985.

Lottery fever had swept the country to the extent that in Shanghai a rat-catching campaign was publicized by offering free lottery tickets to any citizen bringing in a dead rat!

But the love of gambling didn't die with the lotteries. When Shanghai police announced an amnesty in April of that year, sparing gamblers from criminal sentence, over 50,000 gave themselves up. They were mainly mahjong and poker players.

Yet Shanghai gambled on, and a purge on punters was launched by the city authorities in January 1986. All gamblers were ordered to register with the public security bureau, and 8,900 people did so within the month, being more mahjong and card players. They were allowed to go free after being reminded that gambling is prohibited by the Communist Party.

But 7,000 were arrested in raids on 267 gambling dens, according to officials who didn't reveal their fate. The equivalent of £70,000 in wagers was recovered.

A most striking
wager

In 1979 I received one of the most unusual requests of all for a wager – asking for odds against a branch of the Civil Service going on strike!

The writer, whose line of business made it undesirable for his financial well-being that such a strike would take place, was most insistent that his identity should not be revealed, but he wrote, 'To carry on my business I require that the Company Registrars Department of the Department of Trade at London and Cardiff work smoothly. In December 1978 staff at both went on strike for some months bringing business to a standstill. I would like to lay off my risk of this possibility recurring.

'Would your firm be prepared to quote terms against the possibility of another strike recurring at either of the above offices in, say, the next six or twelve months?'

Outspoken punter

Former jockey, TV commentator and journalist Lord Oaksey told me an amusing tale of an off-beat wager.

'I was making a speech once, when I heard someone shout out, "That's enough".

'Irritated, I turned round and said, "Oh, f*** off!", and I was mortified later to discover that he'd only said it because he'd had a bet on how long I'd go on speaking!'

> *A man goes into the bookies on Grand National day with four pebbles and demands to put it all on Red Rum. The manager laughs and tells the man he needs money for a bet. But he insists, so to humour him the manager takes his pebbles and gives him a betting slip.*
>
> *When Red Rum wins the man comes in to claim his winnings so the manager tells the counter clerk to go out in the car park and fill a carrier bag full of gravel for him.*
>
> *The man goes away delighted with his 'winnings' but shortly after returns with a large boulder which he puts on the counter.*
>
> *The manager says, 'Oh no, you can get lost – you must have had a tip for one!'*

Courting a royal winner

Princess Michael of Kent took to the tennis court in January 1986 to win a bet originally struck for a quarter of a million pounds.

The bet originated when the Princess was dining in Antigua with local resident Ron Shaw, who claimed that men were five times better at tennis than women. When fellow diner David Mason, a West End art dealer, disagreed the pair struck a bet of £50,000 at 5/1. The conditions of the bet set Princess Michael against Shaw – with each able to choose a doubles partner.

The Princess selected pro player John McGinley while Shaw was partnered by racing trainer Paul Cole. The Princess and the pro won 6–4, 6–0.

Commented Mason in Nigel Dempster's *Daily Mail Diary*, 'The bet was eventually scaled down considerably but Antiguan children's charities will benefit by a substantial sum thanks to Princess Michael.'

Ear, ear

Anti blood-sports groups angrily protested against
a plan by the Spanish Government to allow punters
to bet on the number of ears won by top matadors
in bullfights.

The scheme required punters to forecast the
performances of fourteen top matadors each
Sunday afternoon and was designed to rival the
football pools.

Ollie's a pound-for-pound winner

Oliver Reed, the hell-raising actor, has always been fond of a gamble – and on one occasion gained pounds by losing pounds.

He won £1,000 during the shooting for one of his many films by losing 12½kg over a two-month spell.

On another occasion, Reed lost a tenner when an acquaintance collected by going into a pub stark naked, drinking a pint, bowing to the ladies present and walking straight out again!

A policeman's lot

During the miners' strike of 1984, squads of police often had to be on hand for long periods of time in case their presence was required.

At a pit near Rotherham on 15 November, reported the *Daily Mirror*, one policeman decided to pass the time by betting his colleagues that he could get a whole orange in his mouth.

To his delight he won the bet.

But triumph turned to panic when he couldn't get the orange out of his mouth!

He was rushed to Rotherham General Hospital where the orange was finally moved, and the constable treated for a dislocated jaw. I bet he copped it from the mandarins at Head Office!

Losing a winner

A Torquay paper reported the sad tale of a rugby player who won £300 from a Teignmouth betting shop.

Sad?

Well, he produced his winning slip at a party during the evening of his win and before he'd been to the shop to collect. A fellow party-goer challenged him to eat it. Somewhat the worse for wear, he promptly chewed it up and swallowed, washing it down with a pint of bitter.

The next morning, horror-struck, he went along to the betting shop to explain what had happened. But they were adamant – no slip, no winnings. Unlike most shops, which would have accepted a copy of the bet, he'd picked one with a different rule.

Said the red-faced rugby player, 'That snack cost me £300, and it didn't even taste very nice.'

One rule for ...

With the Chinese soon to take over the running of Hong Kong there has been some doubt over the future of the thriving racing and betting scene there, particularly as Chairman Deng has reportedly had 32,000 mainland Chinese arrested for gambling.

But, according to Royal Hong Kong Jockey Club chief, General Sir John Archer, racing and gambling should be safe. 'They're against gambling,' he told the *Daily Express* in March 1986, 'But Deng's son came to see the races here and quietly had a ten dollar bet.

'He won.'

Chris-tal clear tip

It's a risky business backing a horse to win the world's most hazardous race – the Grand National. It's even more risky when you back a horse that hasn't even got a name or seen a racecourse at the time you place the bet!

So Chris Liveras must be a very confident punter, because before it even jumped a fence, he backed his own horse to win the Grand National five years running – in 1987,88,89,90 and 91.

The horse is called Mr Chris, and Mr Liveras, chairman of Cleveland company CDL 44 Foods Limited, explains, 'I obtained odds of 200/1 for five years with Ladbrokes at £100 each way for each year, and although Mr Chris has had a little setback I am honestly convinced that he will be placed, if not win, some time during those years in the Grand National.

'Remember, I asked for odds before the horse was even named – never mind racing.'

Don't say we didn't tell you!

Helps you work, rest, play and lose!

Punters had already collected their winnings when the reason for the disqualification of No Bombs, who won a race at Worcester in April 1979, was revealed.

The horse failed a dope test – because he ate part of his lad's Mars Bar just before the race started!

Commentator out-races jockey

It was an unusual race for Walter Swinburn, the jockey who rode Shergar to victory in the Derby.

He was facing only one opponent, a man more usually heard commentating on TV on the outcome of horse races – Julian Wilson.

And the pair were racing over 4,000 feet – on toboggans – for a £2,000 stake.

The great race took place in St Moritz in January 1986 and was decided on the best of three runs down the famed Cresta Run.

Giving away twenty-one years, Wilson, forty-five, was a clear winner with a best time of 48.82 secs against Swinburn's 51.47.

£2,000 richer, Wilson seemed reluctant to offer his opponent the chance of a rematch, saying, 'I'm going to get out while I'm ahead – Walter was catching up with me and improving fast.'

The punter went to a greyhound meeting with fifty pence in his pocket. He put his fifty pence on a 10/1 shot in the first race. It won.
Thinking his luck must be in he put all his winnings on the next race – and won again.
He carried on in this manner until, by the last race, he had £5,129.75 which he put on the odds-on favourite – which led all the way round right until inches from the line, when it fell over and was passed by another dog.
On the way home a friend came over to the punter and said, 'How did you get on?'
The punter replied cheerfully, 'Lost fifty pence!'

20/1/1983.

Dear Sir,

I am 31. and have been Constantly getting into trouble Since the age of 10. and have Spent Some 9 years in prison regretfully most of the cause has been gambling

I wondered what the chances are of you laying me odds of keeping out of trouble over the next 10 or 20 years frankly I would say it was Impossible for me, and most people with officialdom, Such as probation officers etc would say it was Impossible for me to stay out of trouble after the age of 10 the longest break I have had, to 10 month's absolute trouble free

I have a solicitor whom I'm Sure would give you any assistance you may need

No. 2426 30562 30-1048 (RD 3083)

2

In establishing odds. I am thinking of a wager around about £100.

I look forward to your response

yours Sincerely

My goodness,
what a winner

Sixty-nine-year-old George Rhodes from Aldershot was aware he had had a nice win for his 5p seven-horse accumulator, but he wasn't quite sure how much.

Little did he know that he'd won enough to get him into

the *Guinness Book of Records* for landing record-busting odds of over 1,670,000/1!

I went to see George when he was being presented with his cheque, and asked him how he'd found out what he had to come.

'I watched the last race, which Mel's Choice won – he left it pretty late, too – and then rang Hills to check that the bet was definitely on. Mr Don Ready confirmed that it was and asked me how much I thought I'd won. I said, perhaps a few thousand – then he told me that the total amount was well over £90,000!'

After tax, Mr Rhodes collected £86,056.42 for his 5p stake. I asked him what he was going to do with it.

'I'll invest some of it in a new Rolls Royce – my old one is eighteen years old now,' he told me. Mr Rhodes' bet duly appeared in the 1986 edition of the *Guinness Book of Records* under the heading Highest-Ever Odds.

Not his lucky day!

As the seventy-seven-year-old punter triumphantly collected the £360 he had just won for his 25p bet, a young man rushed forward, grabbed the notes out of his hand, and fled.

Said the unlucky man, a retired miner from Market Place, Doncaster, 'I was happy as a sheikh when I won it and suddenly it was gone.'

The Emperor Nero is said to have kicked and killed his pregnant wife Poppaea because she complained that he came home late from the races.

Punters flying high on the right track

Gambling on the move is set to become big business.

As this book went to press Australian National Railways were set to launch a mini casino on their services to and from Alice Springs. A spokesman told me that poker machines and electronic bingo would be introduced on a trial basis and would spread to other routes if they proved popular.

Meanwhile, a new British airline, London Express, were planning something similar on their London to Singapore trip, starting in late '86. Speaking on their behalf, Jeffrey Rayner told me, 'We will definitely have fruit machines on the flights and will probably introduce blackjack and bingo at a later date.'

Travelling light could take on a whole new meaning for unlucky gamblers!

Soccer stars on course

A couple of England soccer captains enjoyed contrasting fortunes with their first racehorses.

Former England star Mike Channon told me how he nearly ruined England skipper Kevin Keegan's training programme after persuading him into racehorse ownership.

A keen racegoer, punter and breeder for years, Channon said, 'After finally persuading Kevin to come into partnership with me owning Man On The Run, I got him to come along to the races. Our horse came stone last – so we got drunk on champagne.'

But current England captain Bryan Robson was far more fortunate, making the winner's enclosure for the first time in April 1986 when his horse Taylormade Boy won at Edinburgh.

Mind you, the win might have caused Robson's club boss, Ron Atkinson of Manchester United, selection problems, for jockey Lindsay Charnock said, 'Robson promised me I could play for United next season if I won on the horse – he'd better keep his word.'

A bubbly rumour

You know how the grapevine works, and how quickly rumours seem to spread – well, Peter Gunn and Alan Dumbreck of the London advertising agency, Doyle Dane Bernbach, bet their financial director Michael Waters a crate of champagne that they could start an untrue rumour which would get back to him within days.

Waters, reported *Campaign*, the advertising business's trade paper, accepted the bet.

Gunn and Dumbreck met a friend from another agency, Abbott Mead Vickers SMS, in a pub and told him they were about to join their own agency's board.

Their friend apparently leaked this story to someone at Waldron Allen Henry and Thompson – who in turn just happened to be meeting another Doyle Dane Bernbach creative team for lunch.

Of course, the DDB team were told the 'news'.

They, in turn, rushed back with the story and complained to their creative director Peter Harold that they hadn't been offered board places!

Harold thought he'd been kept in the dark about the move and immediately tackled Waters about it.

Waters realized he'd just lost a case of champers.

Honesty repaid

An American punter had his honesty acknowledged in a unique manner: the track where he became the one and only punter ever to return the money he had been overpaid on the tote marked the occasion by staging a race in his honour.

Looking for
a fast buck?

'I'm thirty-seven and do a bit of running,' said the letter to a top bookie from a man in South Brent, continuing, 'and I'd like you to give me a price against breaking the three-minute mile.'

The firm passed the man's name on to the Olympic Selection Committee!

Vote yourself
some money

Contesting a council election in Cork City, Ireland, in 1985, Bernard Murphy and his helper John Lennon hit on a great idea to attract votes.

They distributed posters and pamphlets pointing out that the local bookie was quoting Murphy at 33/1 and suggesting that here was a great chance to 'prove them wrong and make some money while you're at it. £165 for £5; £330 for £10. You can vote yourself the money.'

Suddenly, no-hoper Murphy, a newspaper seller and sometime sandwich-board man, became a talking point. The local bookie, Liam Cashman, started taking money for him, and pretty soon Murphy was a mere 9/4 chance.

An independent candidate, one of his main priorities being to abolish gas meters, Murphy polled over 1,000 votes and romped home.

Liam Cashman lost £20,000.

Murphy is now pondering his chances of getting into Parliament. Could he do it? Don't ask Liam Cashman to lay you a price against it!

Long shot?

American gambler Arnold Rothstein produced the biggest winning and losing shots of his legendary career on 4 November 1928. Hoover was elected president, winning Rothstein $500,000 in bets: but Rothstein was fatally shot in the stomach that same day, and never collected his winnings.

Cueing up for a win

Ex-world champion snooker player Steve Davis never used to bet – until he met someone else who did, one Barry Hearn. Hearn teamed up with Steve and started to back him when he played. Before long he had won £26,000 and become Davis' manager.

Now that the odds about Davis winning snooker matches are generally too restricted, Hearn has turned his attentions to betting on horses. And so has Steve.

At Newbury a while ago they nearly gave the bookies a heart attack – and to make matters better they were there as the bookies' guests!

Said Steve, 'We had a £5 each way Heinz bet,' (a bet involving fifty-seven combinations!) 'total stake £570. The bookies were rubbing their hands at the start. They stopped smirking when our first horse went in at 16/1. By the time they were going down for the last race their man was on the phone to his head office sweating buckets!

'All our other selections had been placed, and we only needed a fourth in the last. It was a massive field. We crossed the last in front – but finished fifth. Still, we raked in over £1,000!'

Steve now owns several horses of his own but has another, more eccentric, gambling love. 'I don't normally like gambling unless I'm in control. I like having a bet on a game of Space Invaders.'

● Millwall man Bill Martin bet his life savings of £7,700 on Davis to win the UK Championship – he lost to Alex Higgins.

Q. In which George Bernard Shaw play does the following quote from Colonel Pickering appear, 'I'll bet you all the expenses of the experiment you can't do it'?
A. Pygmalion.

Blind faith

Visiting a recording studio in November 1983 Stevie Wonder, the blind singer, and his companions had been discussing the feats of other unsighted people. Somebody told a story about blues singer Ray Charles, also blind, who apparently once flew a plane.

Song writer Michael Sembello was there. 'When Stevie heard that, he wanted to go one better. He bet the guy who ran the studio that he could race him across a field – in a car!'

Stevie duly got behind the wheel of a car for the race, insisting on taking Sembello along with him. 'I was scared out of my wits. Stevie hadn't a clue what he was doing. He just stuck his foot on the gas and we kept going faster and faster.

'When a lake loomed up I decided it was time to intervene. I wrenched his hands off the wheel, pushed him to the floor, and pulled the handbrake on with all my might. We stopped a foot short of the shore, thank God!'

Sutch a good bet

Self-styled Screaming 'Lord' David Sutch, sometime rock
star and politician extraordinaire, is an old pal whom I first
met when I was a reporter on a local paper in Harrow,
Middlesex. It didn't take long before his gambling instinct
emerged when he founded the infamous Official Monster
Raving Loony Party, and invented a novel method of
paying for his election deposits. He'd back himself to poll a
certain number of votes with the aim of financing his
campaign, and more often than not he would be successful.

Said Sutch, 'It's easy money – everyone writes me off at
these by-elections, but I appeal to the man in the street and
I always fancy my chances of getting a couple of hundred
votes at least. And I'm still convinced that my bandwagon
will eventually grow and that I will be elected to Parliament
– I've even had a bet on myself becoming Prime Minister
at odds of 10,000/1!'

I know – I laid him the bet.

Gnome more betting?

Punters in Queensland, Australia, came in for a lot of criticism when they began to bet on how far a dwarf could be thrown. So they gave up using real people and introduced garden-gnome throwing instead!

However, even this was embroiled in controversy when allegations of gnome-tampering were made – unscrupulous competitors had apparently been drilling holes through their gnomes to make them lighter!

Each way?
Which way?

A group of Irish punters on their way to the Cheltenham Festival races in March 1986, decided to follow the road signs marked 'HR' for Horse Racing. They ended up sixty miles out of their way in Chepstow.

'HR' stood for Holiday Route.

Ante-Post Manager,
William Hill.

Dear Sir,

I should be most grateful if you would give me an Ante-Post price on the following National Sporting Event.

I wish to bet on the possibility of HRH The Princess of Wales giving birth to twins on the occasion of her next (3rd.) confinement, that is to say the delivery subsequent to Prince Harry.

Although the idea may seem premature, you will recall the pressure last time caused by 'people in the know' who were later proved wrong.

I would accept terms of "all in, run or not" and place the bet in your Southampton office should you be in a position to reply with suitable odds.

Yours faithfully,

Steve's forgotten winner

Singer and actor Steve Harley likes a bet, but he tells the tale of the time he totally forgot he'd won nearly £200.

Steve, who follows racing fairly closely, was a great fan of Derby winner Shergar, the horse who was later kidnapped and never seen again. He was upset to see Shergar surprisingly beaten in the St Leger.

'I had a couple of hundred quid on Shergar long before the St Leger, ante-post, but on the day itself something told me to have a fiver each way on Cut Above.

'I watched the race and was so sad for Shergar that I was sitting there depressed for some time before I even found out that Cut Above had won and that I'd backed a 28/1 winner – I'd only been watching Shergar.'

Easy come ... hard go

William Bergstrom from La Grange, Texas walked into Las Vegas' Horseshoe Casino and made history by staking one million dollars on a single roll of the dice!

Bergstrom had made large bets before but nothing of this size, and casino manager Ted Binion recalled, 'He arrived with a battered suitcase full of twenty and fifty dollar bills.'

Bergstrom staked the entire amount on not throwing a seven – and promptly rolled a three and a four to lose the lot! According to Binion, 'He shrugged, said he was hungry and went off to find a Mexican restaurant.'

There is a sad postscript to the tale. Within three months of making the bet, in 1984, Bergstrom was dead, leaving a will saying that he wanted to be remembered as the Phantom Gambler at the Horseshoe Casino.

Another dead cert

There's a tale about a bookmaker who struck a bet for £80, only to see his poor customer immediately fall to the ground.

St John Ambulance men rushed over, laid the man on a stretcher and, after placing a coat over his face, carried him off.

Assuming the punter to be dead, the bookie put the cash for the bet in the bottom of his bag, knowing that if the betting ticket was found on the body a relative might claim any winnings. Two races later the 'dead' punter came running up to the bookie to claim his winnings.

Thinking he had seen a ghost, the bookie fainted!

It later transpired that the man had had an epileptic fit but recovered quickly.

Clough luck!

It was reported in the *Guardian* that Frank Allcock, a director of Nottingham Forest Football Club, had announced his resignation in February 1986, after the club's manager Brian Clough alleged in their programme that Allcock and a former director, Derek Davis, were offering odds of 7/1 against Forest winning at Manchester United in a League match. Ironically, Forest did win – 3–2.

Commented Allcock, 'The article made me look ridiculous. There was merely a conversation in which I offered a bet to a friend.'

• One dedicated Clough fan staked a fiver at odds of 1,000/1 that Brian will eventually become Prime Minister.

Giving Stephenson a rocket

The sensation of the times was Stephenson's Rocket, a
locomotive which sped along at the unheard-of pace of
twenty-four miles per hour. Diminutive George Osbaldeston, known as 'The Squire of All England' and renowned for his willingness to accept any challenge, decided to
bet that he could match that by travelling 200 miles on
horseback in nine hours.

The date was 1831. Osbaldeston was forty-four and had
a crippled leg, but he wagered 1,000 guineas with a
Colonel Charrite that he could achieve the feat. Those
who knew horses scoffed, and bets and side bets were laid
throughout the land as the attempt caught the public
imagination.

Osbaldeston chose the four-mile track at Newmarket
racecourse for his bid, and prepared a team of twenty-eight
horses, each horse to be changed after a circuit.

The timekeepers gathered on a rainy morning and off
went Osbaldeston. He completed the 200 miles in eight
hours forty-two minutes, and allowing for stoppages,
changes and a bit of a struggle with an irritable horse called
Ikey Solomon, he was deemed to have clocked an average
speed of twenty-six miles per hour.

Osbaldeston's offer to wager that he could complete the
distance in eight hours was never taken up.

Tarby's show exposed

I upset the producers of Jimmy Tarbuck's popular TV quiz show *Winner Takes All* by revealing how contestants could cheat their way to victory. The show offers them a series of possible answers to the questions. Each answer has a set of odds against it and the contestants stake an amount of money that they will guess correctly. If they do they receive back the appropriate amount of winnings.

However, with the show involving two separate pairs of contestants, I realized that the total winning odds available to each set of contestants must be equal to be fair. Therefore, by keeping a mental note of the total winning odds available to the first pair of contestants the second would be able to deduce the answer to their final question by totting up what the previous ones had added up to. Don't worry if you can't quite follow that – just accept that it's true!

When I contacted the programme to explain my theory they tried to excuse themselves in several ways before inviting me up to a recording of the programme. Whether they ever changed the format to eliminate the discrepancy I never did discover – and I certainly couldn't bring myself to watch the programme any more to find out!

However, when I later interviewed Jimmy Tarbuck he was very friendly. Jimmy, whose father was a bookie, told me his favourite gambling story was a true tale about his mother. She had little interest in betting, but decided one day to back a horse.

'She looked at the odds on the board in the betting shop and heard the commentator announce, "It's ten to one bar six". Not knowing that "bar six" was a racing term meaning "apart from those already mentioned", my mum demanded to back – Bar Six!'

Mae be a winner

One of the most unlikely requests for a bet ever received by Ladbrokes was from the punter who wanted to wager that when actress Mae West died, it would be discovered that she was a man!

That Singhking feeling

Graham Singh rang me from Darwin, Australia in July 1983 to say that he wanted to put $2,000 on himself driving a car for six miles – under water.

Mr Singh, a diver, was deadly serious. He and a team of other divers were to drive a four-wheel drive Toyota owned by the Territory Driving Service, and adapted to work under water, from Darwin to an island some six miles off the coast.

The previous world record for such a feat was, he told me, 130 feet, but they were convinced they could go the whole six miles, even though they would be driving along a sea bed some 120 feet down.

In practice runs, said Graham, they had done 200 yards, but their attempt was being taken seriously enough for the *Guinness Book of Records* to nominate a Darwin councillor to adjudicate on their behalf.

Well, he was supposed to call back to confirm the date of the attempt, but never did. I tried ringing him to find out how they'd got on, but I never could get through and I only hope they didn't come to any harm in the effort.

Happy anniversary!

Lincoln bookmaker Willy White took a £1,000 bet with a difference in May 1984 – from a twenty-eight-year-old man betting that his marriage would last for seven years! The backer wanted to keep his identity secret in case his wife found out.

White offered even money on a marriage between a couple aged thirty or over lasting seven years without a break up or either partner admitting an affair. . . .

. . . Soccer fan Mike Dart bet his wedding on the result of an FA Cup match.

Twenty-three-year-old Mike bet that he would propose to his girlfriend Liz Robinson if his team, Reading, beat Huddersfield in a third round replay in January 1986.

They did, and in the stand, he did. Twenty-seven-year-old Liz immediately said yes. . . .

. . . Gambling-mad Terry Nichol wasn't going to let a little thing like getting married interfere with his hobby.

So the thirty-seven-year-old Trowbridge man arranged the ceremony in September 1983, within sprinting distance of a betting shop.

Minutes before the ceremony he dashed in to place a bet and seconds after the registrar had finished joining Terry and Janet Flonn in matrimony he shot back there for the result.

For the duration of the reception Terry was in and out of the shop. 'There's a race every fifteen minutes and I didn't want to miss any. I'm a reasonable man but I didn't see why the wedding should get in the way of my punting,' he told reporters.

His wife said, 'I don't mind so long as he keeps winning.'

His bookie, Geoffrey Blake, gave him a £10 free bet as a wedding present, so he probably *doesn't* keep on winning!

Hare-racing experience

Gamblers on greyhound racing in America no longer wager on their selection getting closest to a mechanical hare, as is the case in England and most other places where the sport is popular.

Explained an American official, George Dewey, at the World Greyhound Racing Federation's conference in 1985, 'We are trying to eliminate hare and rabbit from our vocabulary to satisfy the Humane Society. We use a big white plastic bone with a ribbon attached. The shout now is "Here comes Boney!"'

Titanic sinks opposition

American gambler 'Titanic' Thompson was a tricky customer when it came to betting. He bet some Broadway characters he could drive a golf ball 300 yards – and did it off a hill with a 300-yard drop.

Then he bet Washington sports writers that he could throw a walnut further than star baseball pitcher Walter Johnson. He won by inserting a lead slug in his walnut!

Starting young

Toddler Shelley Bell may be Britain's youngest successful tipster.

At the age of fourteen months in June 1985 her dad Steven sat her on his knee and said, 'Find Daddy a winner.'

Shelley, of Blackburn, Lancs, stabbed at the racing page of his paper with a pen and came up with four horses – which all won.

Steven, twenty-eight, backed the four in a 50p-each-way accumulator and relieved Corals of £1,330!

●*Author's note* My first son, Steeven, was born just before midnight on 20 August 1980. Delighted, I said to my wife Sheila as the baby arrived, 'Here comes young Sharpo.' The next day my company sponsored one of the most important races of the season, the William Hill Sprint Championship, and in it was a horse called Sharpo. I plunged a few quid on, and Sharpo won, as it also did for the next two years.

So perhaps the hours-old Steeven Sharpe can claim to be the youngest successful tipster!

> *The unlucky punters had lost on five consecutive races.*
> *With just one event remaining, one punter turned to the*
> *other and said, 'That priest over there – he's been making*
> *a sign over one horse in each race, then backing it. And*
> *he's had five winners.'*
> *The punters decided to watch the priest and back the horse*
> *he made the sign over with all their remaining cash.*
> *The horse shot ahead of its opponents and was well clear*
> *with only yards to run when it suddenly collapsed.*
> *Disappointed, the punters went and spoke to the priest,*
> *explaining why they had decided to back the horse.*
> *Replied the priest, 'That's the trouble with you atheists –*
> *you can't tell the difference between a blessing and the*
> *last rites!'*

It ain't
nessi–ssarily so!

One of the most popular unusual bets I have ever offered prices for is whether the Loch Ness Monster will be proved to exist.

You can have 100/1 against the Natural History Museum admitting to the existence of a creature previously unknown, and responsible for the 'Nessie' sightings, within a year of placing your bet.

In early 1983, we suddenly took a whole heap of bets and reduced the odds to 25/1 when respected scientist Adrian Shine reported in the *New Scientist* magazine that his investigations in Loch Ness had 'produced data consistent with the presence of large animals.'

Sadly, conclusive proof is as yet unforthcoming and the odds have drifted back to 100/1. Even the manager of the betting shop nearest to Loch Ness, Angus McCray, says he is unsure as to whether there is a monster, but adds 'We used to have a regular punter in here who actually set up camp on the shore for two years searching for the monster. Come to think of it, I haven't seen him recently . . .'

Splott on!

The manager of the betting shop in Splott, Cardiff, was suspicious of the £50 note a punter handed over. But by the time the police had been called in and confirmed the note was forged, the punter's horse had won. So the shop paid him his winnings, less £50 to compensate – and then the police nicked him!

A little bet of nookie

Gambling has given star ventriloquist Roger de Courcey more than his fair share of headaches – and it is all the fault of his stage partner, Nookie Bear.

After winning the *New Faces* TV talent show, de Courcey decided to buy himself a racehorse which he not unnaturally named after his constant teddy-bear companion.

Nookie Bear first caused him problems by winning a race. 'He won at odds of 14/1, and I didn't have a penny on him! In fact I was lying by a swimming pool on holiday in Spain when someone came up to me, showed me a paper with the result in and said "It must be drinks on you tonight, Roger". I was choked!'

Then Nookie Bear caused him problems by half-winning a race. The horse was racing at Fakenham, where there was no photo finish camera, and the judge decided that he had only dead-heated with another runner, James Seymour.

'We won by half a length,' Roger told me, still fuming at the memory. 'It was diabolical that such a course shouldn't have photo-finish facilities. It cost me a nice few bob' (stakes are halved when a horse dead-heats) 'as I'd a couple of large bets on the horse at my local bookies – and advised everyone else I knew in there to back him, too.'

In the next day's papers, even the *Sporting Life* was on his side. 'The absence of such equipment probably cost Nookie Bear an outright victory,' said the paper. This further enraged de Courcey who nearly got himself banned for life. 'I went out with the express intention of buying a Polaroid camera and sending it to the course, but I was advised that racing authorities are not renowned for having a sense of humour and that I would be better off just forgetting it.'

Finally, Nookie Bear caused him problems by nearly winning a race. 'Comedian Jim Davidson and some other friends went to Windsor one day to represent me when I couldn't make it to see the horse run. I hadn't advised them to back Nookie Bear, and he started at 33/1. But as they came over the last he was in front, and Jim told me later they were calling me all the names under the sun. Fortunately he finished second – and saved my life!'

'Allo, 'allo, 'allo!

Policemen anxious to know how their bets had got on were accused of 'dishonest' practices when their habit of ringing up Raceline, British Telecom's racing results service, was discovered.

Scotland Yard's B6 communications branch launched an investigation when it was noticed that phone bills in London police stations were soaring. The branch issued a strongly worded memo in July 1985 saying, 'It is clear that many practices have been adopted which are not only wasteful of resources, or even dishonest, but also very costly.

'Typical is the persistent use of recorded services such as racing information, weather reports, Dial-a-Disc, Recipe of the Day, and the like.'

Funny – I'd have thought they'd have been in favour of anything which increased the old bill!

Budgeting for a win

Bookie Keith Little was astonished when the punter who'd asked for a bet on the Budget proved correct in all four of his predictions.

He was even more astonished when it was revealed that the man was a chef at the House of Commons!

However, an enquiry ruled that he could have had no access to a budget leak. Nonetheless, he accurately predicted that car tax, petrol, cigarettes and spirits would all go up in the March 1985 budget. He won £3,645. Insiders said it was the third successive year that the chef, Stephen Farrar, and his colleagues had collected.

Little, a Chingford bookie, said, 'I figured the bloke must have a crystal ball. I had been expecting a small flutter – I was amazed when he brought out a stake of £270.'

You dirty rat!

Brian Turner of Devon delighted punters but angered animal lovers when he invented the sport of mouse racing in 1983.

Brian began organizing meetings at Honiston's Three Tuns Hotel, and enthusiastic gamblers turned up in force for the ten-strong races run over a thirteen-foot jumping course. Up to £200 an evening was changing hands, and the sport began to catch on elsewhere.

Then someone 'ratted' on Brian – a cheesed-off punter, perhaps – and the RSPCA decided that they weren't happy. 'There has been a definite increase in mouse racing recently and we are very concerned,' said a spokesman. 'Mouse racing is illegal and it is possible that either we or the police will be taking legal action.'

If at first . . .

The despair of punters and the delight of bookies – that was little-known racehorse Oureone. Between December 1976 and November 1983 in Sydney, Australia, the mare set a new world record by racing 124 times – without ever winning!

Punter riot
at Derby

Newmarket-based jockey Paul D'Arcy went to India to ride in the Calcutta Derby in 1985, but ended up fleeing for his life when things went wrong.

'All the stable lads went on strike so the horses failed to turn up for the first few races on the card on Derby Day,' explained Paul. 'Racegoers who had paid to get in were kept in the dark about what was happening.

'It was some time before the Turf Club officials announced over the PA system that racing was cancelled, and some of the crowd just went wild. 'They started throwing a few chairs and TV sets around. It looked as if it could turn very nasty so I jumped into a taxi and left quickly to get the first flight back home. I'd had enough by that time.'

Helfried's tough luck

As all gamblers soon find out, the only time you ever win is when you don't really need to – or even want to.

And Austrian teacher Helfried Luck discovered the truth of that old adage with a vengeance when he decided to give his pupils a practical demonstration in what a mug's game gambling really is.

Thirty-nine-year-old Helfried planned to demonstrate by losing £20 on a one-armed bandit in a casino in Graz, Austria, in January 1986.

Inevitably, he won – a mere £150,000!

Commented Helfried, 'I only played the machine to prove to my pupils that gambling doesn't pay. My name is Luck and I've been lucky all my life – but now I've got a lot of explaining to do to my class!'

Baa-rmy bet

On The Buses star Bob Grant is a little sheepish about the £100 bet he lost to pantomime promoter Joe Weston-Webb at the end of 1985. Bob was appearing in Joe's promotion of *Cinderella* and the pair went out to plug the show, driving a 'Smurfmobile' car which was playing music through loud-speakers.

As they drove through the country lanes with Smurf music blaring, Weston-Webb said, 'We noticed sheep in a field getting quite excited and running towards the music. I argued that this was because Smurfs were related to sheep and they recognized the Smurf singing. Bob Grant thought I was crazy and we struck a bet for £100.' To settle the bet thirty sheep were driven into the De Montfort Hall, Leicester, and penned on a raised platform in one row across the stalls with their backs to the stage, closely guarded by two sheep dogs. At the set moment the curtains were to open and the Smurfs would begin dancing to their music. If the sheep turned to watch, Joe would win, if not then Bob would collect.

Ewe can guess the result for yourself! As sheep are renowned for gambolling the bet was as good as won – and Bob Grant found himself shorn of £100!

Nick loses his shirt

Rock star Nick Heyward literally lost his shirt when one of his singles flopped. He was so confident that *Warning Sign* would hit the Top Ten that he struck a wager with drummer Blair Cunningham – if it didn't he'd strip off in public.

The single sank without trace, and Heyward lost his nerve. He went half the way, appearing topless in the *Sun*.

◇ 95 ◇

Ghoul gamblers

New York lottery officials were forced to close the betting when thousands of bets were placed on one number.

The possible payout on number 1139 had reached over £3 million – and the shocked lottery organizers realized that the number represented the exact time at which the Challenger space shuttle had exploded in the sky, killing all seven astronauts on board, just two days earlier in January 1986.

Slamming 'morbid' punters for trying to make money out of human suffering, the lottery officials revealed that the same thing had happened in 1983 when Americans plunged their cash on the flight number of the Korean jet blasted out of the sky by Russian fighters.

A lunar-tic bet

Very early in the 1960s a client wrote in to our Head Office, 'I wish to bet £10 that a man will reach the moon within ten years.'

When the odds-makers had stopped laughing at such an idiotic request they decided to offer David Threlfall 1,000/1 to his money – and just to add a further safeguard, Hills stipulated that the man reaching the moon must be alive, remembers Roy Sutterlin, then a director of the company.

On 21 July 1969 Neil Armstrong took his 'one small step for a man and one giant leap for mankind' on the surface of the moon. It was a giant leap for punters all right, and Eamonn Andrews handed over a cheque for £10,000 to Mr Threlfall, courtesy of William Hill.

Many other punters who had taken advantage of the generous odds also collected, amongst them Professor Archibald Roy of Glasgow University's astronomy department who had staked £20 in 1964 at which time the odds were 60/1.

There is a sad postscript to the tale. Apparently Mr Threlfall purchased a new car with his winnings, and died in an accident in it. That is the story – perhaps someone could confirm or, I hope, deny it.

Meanwhile, Hills were more cautious when punters started to ask for odds against a man walking on the surface of Mars and only offered 100/1. The timespan is now up, so they got some of their cash back.

Building up to a bet

In 1962, workmen employed on the site of the early warning station being constructed at Fylingdales Moor, Yorkshire, complained they were bored in their spare time as there was nothing to do in the bleak countryside where they were living for the duration of the contract.

So Honest Jack Gill, as he became known, opened up a betting shop on the site – and did a roaring trade; 'It adds a fillip to the day,' a workman was reported as saying at the time.

Winner's a loser

Punters would be well advised not to try to back the winner of what is allegedly the world's oldest horse race.

By tradition, first prize in the Kiplingcotes Derby, run near Hull since 1519, is the interest from money invested by a benefactor last century, which is about £20. But the second prize is made up of the sum of the £4 entry fees for the race, run over a four-and-a-half-mile farmland course. As the race usually attracts a large field, the runner-up ends up with a larger prize than the winner – must make for an interesting tussle at the finish with riders battling desperately to be beaten!

Gamble that mist out

Many years ago, so the tale goes, English politician Horatio Bottomley owned a racing stable and thought he'd clean up by taking a few thousand pounds off the Belgians.

He entered six of his better horses in a minor race at Blankenberg where they seemed certain to have the race between them.

To fox the bookies he bet varying amounts under different names on each of his entries, but his jockeys were under strict instructions as to who should finish where.

The course was close to the coast, and as the race went off in blew a thick sea mist which totally obscured the vision of spectators and jockeys – the jockeys lost touch with each other, nobody knew where anybody else was, the wrong result inevitably came up and Bottomley lost a fortune!

> *It was the punter's sixty-sixth birthday on 6 June, the sixth month of 1966.*
> *Checking the racing pages he noticed that in the sixth race, horse number six was called Lucky Six, and quoted at 6/1.*
> *He rushed to the bookies to put £6 on it, thinking his luck must be in.*
> *It came sixth.*

By George

The biggest single winner in an American state lottery at time of going to press was George Wittkowski, a Chicago printer who won $40 million in 1984.

In January 1985, fifty-nine-year-old New York bricklayer Pasquale Consalvo became the second biggest winner when he landed a $30 million win.

Family and friends took his work clothes and boots out to the dustbin!

Guto's gamble

Early in the eighteenth century, Welshman Guto Nyth-Bran thought up an unusual wager to win back a great deal of money that a friend of his had lost on a bet.

Guto decided to race against a horse in Cardiganshire in a cross-country event, and hit on a novel form of training – he slept the night prior to the race on a local manure heap!

Guto won the race, got the money back for his friend but ultimately lost the greatest stake of all – his life. After

repeating his victory over another horse, he met an untimely end when wives and girlfriends of his acquaintances clapped him so enthusiastically on the back after he had finished the race, exhausted, that he promptly expired!

Incidentally, a man-against-horse marathon is now held annually in Llanwrtyd Wells, but since its inception in 1980 the horse has yet to lose.

● In 1984, while he was there for a poker tournament, Professional player Amarillo Slim of Texas offered to stake $50,000 that he could beat the horse Topham Tavern, the winner of the Isle of Man's Manx Derby, in a hundred-yard dash along Douglas beach. Despite being fifty-three years old, such was his gambling reputation that he found no takers.

Racetrack's ex-Rey

Working as a clerk with the Tote at a Florida racetrack in May 1984, Rey Gallegos hit the wrong button on his machine and punched up a £7,850 ticket for a £785 forecast bet.

The punter refused to buy the ticket, leaving Rey responsible and sweating on a debt of nearly £8,000, for which he would certainly have been liable: with the race under orders right then, there was no time to cancel the bet.

Two minutes later Rey was £31,307 richer as the favourite beat a 37/1 shot by a neck to land the forecast for him!

Russian in for a bet

I visited Russia in 1985 with a group of non-gamblers. They knew nothing about football, either, but couldn't resist visiting the world-famous Moscow Dynamo soccer stadium to see a match.

I managed to talk them all into betting a few roubles with me at long odds on Moscow Dynamo's opponents, another Moscow side, Torpedo. With my superior soccer knowledge, I was well aware that they were no-hopers.

Torpedo won easily. I lost all my holiday roubles and was reduced to dealing in the black market to get them back!

At the time we were visiting, Mr Gorbachev had just clamped down on drinking and many of the Moscow bars were dry. Our party smuggled vast amounts of booze into our hotel bar and sat down for a harmless game of cards for small change. When a waitress rushed over and burst into hysterical ranting and raving we thought she was up in arms about the booze. Not a bit of it – it was our game of snap, with its penny, franc and rouble stakes which she and apparently the rest of the hotel staff objected to. We were nearly slung out on to the streets!

There has been enormous betting interest on the last two occasions that the Russian leader has changed – and on both occasions Hill's resident Kremlin-watcher has been spot-on with his odds.

Says Mike Cowtan, 'This was a bet I first introduced when Andropov died, and I made Chernenko favourite to replace him, which he did. Chernenko didn't last long and I immediately offered prices with Gorbachev as favourite – now I get calls from journalists asking for information on the Russian hierarchy.'

It is not only Russian leaders Cowtan will bet on. He's offering prices on the next elected American leader after President Reagan, making Robert Redford a 50/1 chance. And he also thinks Clint Eastwood could well be a live candidate for the highest honour by the early to mid-nineties.

Tanner tip

In the 1870s, Lord Falmouth was far and away the top owner of race horses in England – but he never gambled.

He broke that rule on just one occasion: Mrs Scott, the wife of his trainer, bet him sixpence that his filly Queen Bertha would win the Oaks.

Lord Falmouth accepted the bet – and Queen Bertha duly won the Oaks.

The noble Lord paid up, having the sixpence set in diamonds before he presented it to Mrs Scott!

Shelling out?

Betting on tortoise racing is big business in Singapore. It's an action-packed sport with one-hundred-metre sprints over in as little as forty minutes!

The flying competitors race up a straight track divided into lanes by wooden planks. Gambling is heavy, and spectator excitement unrestrained.

The tortoises are carefully selected and brought over to Singapore from nearby tourist islands, such as Sentosa. They weigh in at about 1½lbs and carry their owners' colours on their backs – literally so, as they're generously daubed with colourful paints to distinguish one from the other.

They are seriously trained before meetings. Some trainers starve their protégés for a few days before a race, on the grounds that this will make them speed off looking for food when the flag goes up.

Others claim that by putting them in water and encouraging them to splash their limbs about it will stimulate movement and tone them up, ready to dash off at a dramatic pace. They are fed all sorts of 'secret' concoctions aimed at making them go faster.

The races, run from three to one hundred metres, are full of incident. It is not unusual for the animals to sprint off for a while – then appear to fall sound asleep as the rest of the field ambles past! Other runners have been known to climb over the dividing planks and jump lanes – or even to turn round and sprint back the other way.

Q. **In which year did betting shops become legal in England, Scotland and Wales?**
A. **1961.**

Food for thought

An angry row erupted between New Zealand and Australian rugby-union followers when two All Blacks players alleged that their team was deliberately poisoned so that bets on Australia would be won.

All Blacks skipper Stu Wilson and winger Bernie Fraser made the allegations about the crucial deciding match of the 1980 series in Australia in their book *Ebony And Ivory*.

Wilson said he believed that food poisoning, which affected twenty-five of the twenty-eight-strong New Zealand party, was linked with a betting plunge on the Aussies and said, 'If he (the bettor) had seen our boys agonizing through the night, queuing up to use two receptacles, he'd have gone out and doubled his bet.'

Australia won the game and the series, but their rugby football union described the allegations as 'utterly ridiculous'.

Weighing up the odds

Former Conservative Prime Minister Edward Heath may be surprised to learn that his stomach has been the subject of some weighty wagers!

Asked by the *Daily Star* newspaper in April 1986 what MPs do in the House of Commons when proceedings become a little tedious, ex-Labour MP Robert Kilroy-Silk answered, 'We talk amongst ourselves and place bets on the size and weight of Ted Heath's belly.'

Dear Sir or Madam,

In the BBC where I work I am informed that you Lay prices on virtually anything. Well I would like to know what price you would Lay me to a £50 stake on my son who is 2yrs 3mths old becoming a professional footballer. Its a bet which who knows your company might not be in existance when the time comes but this is a genuine enquiry So I would be grateful if you would give it some consideration.

Yours Sincerely

Robertson's moon shot

As an insurance broker, Willie Robertson was well aware of the importance of having the odds in his favour. So when Keith Moon, the manic drummer from The Who, offered him an unusual bet whereby he could pick up a substantial amount of business, Robertson hesitated only briefly – before taking off his shoes and socks and walking barefoot along the top of the table through the fillet steaks being eaten by diners at a nearby table in Tramps, the fashionable London night club!

Said Robertson, 'I must have had a little too much to drink, so I took on the wager. I got a bit of a ticking off from the management, but I also got the business – and Keith bought those poor people some more steaks.'

Bookie bashing

A winning punter is a happy person. But if his bookie seems unlikely to pay out he can rapidly become the opposite.

A 'welshing' bookie discovered the truth of this in the autumn of 1868, with dire consequences.

A journalist of the time, James Greenwood, witnessed at Alexandra Park an incident unlikely to be repeated at Royal Ascot.

The fleeing bookmaker in question, 'in a black wide-awake cap, with the regular betting-man's pouch slung at his side', was being pursued by an angry crowd. He was brought down, and regained his feet only to fall once more. 'He was up again, however, without his hat and his face a hideous patch of crimson, but hustled towards the gate, plunging like a madman to escape the fury of his pursuers; but the policeman blocked his way and they caught him again and some punched his face while others tore his clothes.'

Making a desperate effort, the man was once more on the verge of escape, only for a fellow bookie to fling a stool at him, bringing him to earth yet again. Finally, a mounted policeman intervened and 'the poor tattered wretch, ghastly white and streaming with blood, was hauled out and dragged away insensible, with his head hanging and his legs trailing in the dust, amid the howling and horrible execrations of five thousand Englishmen.'

A couple of days later a local paper reported, 'The unfortunate man who so rashly roused the fury of the sporting fraternity at Alexandra Races, is dead.'

Gone for gold

There was little danger of the bookies having to pay up when they offered odds against the highly rated American athlete Steve Prefontaine winning a gold medal at the Olympics – unknown to them, he'd been dead for a number of months!

Homing in on Martina

Tired of hearing praise heaped on the head of Martina Navratilova, tennis ace Vitas Gerulaitis declared that the women's champion wasn't a patch on male players – in fact, 'She'd never beat even the hundredth best male player – I'd bet my house on that!' And for a while it looked like Martina was rising to the bait in an effort to beat New Yorker Vitas literally out of house and home.

Vitas came up with the wager in August 1984, at which time the player ranked one hundred was South African Derek Tarr. Apparently needled by the challenge, Martina commented, 'Vitas could regret that remark – if I got to pick the surface I'd have a shot.'

Later, perhaps realising that she had her reputation to lose and precious little to gain, Martina pulled out of the contest, saying, 'It's ridiculous. You don't mix middle-weights with heavyweights.'

●In September 1973 in America, former top-rank tennis player Bobbie Riggs, then in his mid-fifties, staked $100,000 that he could beat women's champion Billie Jean King. Over 30,000 people turned up to see Billie Jean thrash Riggs (who a year earlier had beaten Margaret Court) by 6–4, 6–3, 6–3.

Yankee's dandy

Not one punter or tipster fancied the chance of the runner who finished fourth in the 2.15 at Lingfield Races on 21 December 1985.

For fourth position was occupied by Yankee – a greyhound!

The dog was at the races with owner Mrs Violet Cohen of Hove when he suddenly decided he could do better than the seventeen horses in the event. Said Mrs Cohen's husband, Sid, 'He dragged my wife off her feet and broke the leash.

'Poor Vi collapsed with shock and didn't see Yankee overtake most of the field.'

HE'D HAVE WON IF HE HADN'T STOPPED AT EVERY ONE!

A keen gambling man on holiday in Italy is passing the Vatican. He decides to pop in to see the Pope but is told by an aide that His Holiness is unavailable.

He tries on three consecutive days, getting the same answer. On the last attempt the aide finally tells the man, 'Sadly, the Pope has passed on, but we are not releasing the news to the world until next week.'

The man returns home and rushes straight to his local bookmaker and takes odds of 100/1 against the Pope dying before the end of the week.

On his way out he sees an old man sobbing his heart out. 'What's the matter?' he asks. The man tells him he has lost everything and can't afford to pay his bills.

'Don't tell anyone, but I've got a certainty for you – I'll lend you a tenner – put it on the Pope being announced dead by the end of the week.'

Sure enough, the announcement of the Pope's demise is made and the man goes to the betting shop to collect his winnings. On the way out he meets the old man, who is still sobbing his heart out. 'What's the matter? You must have won a lot of money. Didn't you put the bet on?'

'Yes, I did,' said the old man, 'but I doubled up with the Archbishop of Canterbury!'

Weather it's a certainty?

It seemed the certainty of all time – a punter had written asking for odds that it would rain in Manchester!

However, the client, whom I came to know quite well through a spirited correspondence, had made the bet a little tricky for himself. 'On St Swithin's Day, 15 July 1984, between noon and 6 p.m. over central Manchester there will be thundery showers and heavy rain. This incident will be reported by the television news.'

He lost thirty quid on that one. But he bounced back: 'During the first fourteen days of August 1984, Britain will be subject to a minor earthquake measuring a minimum of 1 on the Richter scale, caused probably by a slip in the Dinorwic Fault in Wales.'

After further thought he amended his bet and narrowed the day of the earthquake down to 12 August, adding that there would be heavy rain and thunderstorms in Manchester to coincide!

Unfortunately we couldn't lay odds for this one as an earthquake could have led to loss of life.

Our punter then went on to bet another £30 that it would rain in Manchester on 12 August, and a further £40 for 26 August. Sadly for him he'd discovered the only way to prevent rainfall in Manchester – put money on it!

I wrote to the punter, who lives near Manchester, to ask for his permission to use his name here. He declined, but did ask cheekily, 'Are you accepting any wagers on how well your book will sell?'

Hurricane blown out

Former world snooker champion Alex 'Hurricane' Higgins was delighted when the £400 treble bet he'd put on the horses came up. He reckoned he had £6,000 to come.

But Alex, who placed the bet while playing an exhibition match in Ireland in 1983, never received a penny – the bookie, Noel O'Loughlin, wasn't licensed.

And it was small comfort to Higgins that O'Loughlin was later fined £25 for conducting business without a licence.

Elvis lives on

Elvis Presley lives on – at least in the minds of his fans, two of whom seem to have taken their fervour to extremes.

One, R. Reynolds, sent a fiver to his bookie to bet that 'Elvis Presley will descend to earth in a flying saucer and re-enter the human form that he left, so that his millions of fans will be able to see him perform again.'

And another, a Surrey lady, will receive £25,000 on the day that she has tea with the reincarnated Elvis.

Ruth is stranger than fiction!

Mrs Ruth E. Norman, a widow from California and the founder of the Unarius Educational Foundation, has invested thousands of pounds in recent years gambling that aliens will land in her backyard.

One of her letters to her English bookie read, 'Dear Friend, since the spacecraft will land on my property on 23 December you will therefore have approximately one and a half million dollars to send me.'

Sadly, the landing lights can't have been working properly, for she's still waiting for the spacecraft to show up! . . .

. . . Clearly on the same wavelength as Mrs Norman was the gentleman from Leighton Buzzard who wanted to stake enough to win himself £1 million by proving his theory which states that 'scientists of the world will agree that UFOs have appeared to us as a result of mankind's interference with God's natural laws'. . . .

The dream Derby

Once of the heaviest Derby gambles of all time was on a horse which, having no form, to all intents and purposes had no right even to be in the race.

In 1967, Royal Palace was a hot favourite. An unconsidered outsider, quoted at 500/1, was a horse called El Mighty. A few days before the race the *News of the World* carried a story about one of their readers who claimed to have had a vivid dream in which he 'saw' El Mighty storming past the post in first place in the Derby.

That article sparked a major plunge with all bookmakers on the horse and within a matter of hours liabilities on the horse ran into millions.

Hill's director at the time, Roy Sutterlin, recalled, 'We were absolutely inundated with bets on the horse both from the public and from other bookmakers wanting to hedge their liabilities. El Mighty went from an outsider with nothing to recommend him to being the single largest liability we have had before or since on any one individual horse.'

By the day of the race, El Mighty had been backed down to sixth favourite for the race in a field of twenty-two.

The race went off at 3.44 – nine minutes late – and there was tense silence in Hill's Trade Room as everyone clustered around a TV set.

With two furlongs to go, El Mighty was leading the field. But as the horses thundered for the line, El Mighty finally found the pace too hot: he started to weaken and drop back – and with that the dream gamble died too, and El Mighty ended up where he should always have been according to the form book – in eighteenth place.

Well-fancied Royal Palace won the race – and for once the bookies were delighted that the favourite had won.

Caught at the last

In 1921 jockey Harry Atherton Brown undertook a wager to catch a salmon and ride a winner within an hour.

He caught the salmon – which weighed 44lbs and was the best catch of the season – and shortly after was leading by ten lengths at the final fence in a chase at Hereford when his horse fell!

Two architects were digging out in the desert when they came across an ancient body. After a swift examination one turned to the other and said, 'This is definitely a suicide.'
'How can you tell?' asked his companion.
'Well, he has a note clutched in his hand – it says "500 win Goliath"!'

Tim names his stake

Tim Osborn ran out of money during a poker hand, so he placed a unique bet to cover his stake – if he lost he'd change his name to Margaret Thatcher.

He lost, but not before he'd had to cover another round of betting by offering to shave his head!

Said twenty-one-year-old jobless Tim of Clifton, Bristol, to a national newspaper reporter, 'I went upstairs and shaved all my hair off. The next day I went down to my solicitors and had a change-of-name deed drawn up.'

On the ball

Way back in the eighteenth century, when the fastest means of travel was by horseback, the Duke of Queensberry, then the Earl of March, made what seemed an impossible wager – a bet that he could send a letter fifty miles in an hour.

The Duke won the bet by hiring a team of twenty-four men, all expert catchers and throwers, whom he spaced out at regular intervals over a measured distance of land. He then placed the letter inside a cricket ball and had his men throw the ball from hand to hand until it had travelled fifty miles in total.

Driving ambition

If you won £80,000 you wouldn't spend all those winnings trying to win a car, would you?

Well, perhaps it says something about the difference between markets in the East and West that two young Hungarians who, in January 1985, won £83,000 in the country's biggest ever soccer pools payout, reinvested nearly all of it in lottery bonds offering cars as prizes.

Hell on earth!

One might imagine that such an august body as the Churches' Council would be the last organization to promote the setting up of a 'gambling hell'!

Yet this is just what they did in a submission to the Royal Commission on Gambling, appointed in 1976.

The Commission reported that the Council put forward, in oral evidence from the Reverend Gordon Moody, a plan for two kinds of betting office, the first 'for people who simply want to have a bet and go away again', and the second for punters who, because of either innate desire or irredeemable conditioning, wanted to take part in continuous betting or, as the Churches' Council put it, to 'get into the action'.

'They would have all the facilities needed by punters . . . but entry would be restricted, either by requiring the owners to charge for admission or by making them operate as clubs, like casinos.'

The Council described these betting offices as a 'gambling hell', said the Commission, which wasn't too keen on the idea. 'We think it underestimates the practical and other difficulties which a two-tier system of off-course betting would create.'

A funny thing happened
at the bookies (2)

The ragingly drunk punter in the Edinburgh shop had been out of luck all afternoon. After the seventh consecutive loser his patience snapped. He dashed over to the results marker – and bit him on the backside! . . .

. . . As each race began, the Blackpool betting shop manager shouted 'Get 'em off!' to his counter clerk as an indication that she should accept no more bets. One day he called his usual message – and a punter immediately dropped his trousers and underpants and stood in the middle of the shop wearing just a wide grin. . .

. . . A well-known charity collector went into the shop in Kent and whispered to the manager that he wanted £200 on a horse. Fine, said the manager, where's the money? 'Look in the dustbin,' said the man. The manager went outside and found in the dustbin a bag containing £200 of silver and copper. . .

. . . A punter walked up to the counter of a betting shop in Stockton-on-Tees in March 1986 and handed over a bet on a horse called Deep Trouble. At that precise moment, a car crashed into the betting shop!

Fortunately, no one was hurt – but the horse lost.

The *Sunday Times* reported the case of the hermit who wagered with villagers near Caracas in Venezuela that he could hypnotize and tame a marauding jaguar.
The jaguar savaged the hermit to death.

Toss you for it!

Little did the two noble gentlemen, about to toss a coin for the right to name a horse race after themselves, realize that the descent of the coin would ensure immortality for one of them.

Up went the coin with both of them watching it closely.

Down it came – on the right side for Lord Derby!

The unlucky loser was Sir Charles Bunbury.

Blackjack ace trumped

Ken Uston, senior vice president of the Pacific Stock Exchange, astonished his colleagues by announcing he was quitting one world of finance for another – he was going to become a professional card player.

And so successful did the Harvard-educated blackjack expert become that he is today a millionaire – and no one will let him play in their casino!

He once had to resort to playing in disguise, but was recognized and thrown out.

Uston, who has written books on card-counting, the system of keeping track of all the cards played, went to the courts after he was banned from playing in Nevada and Atlantic City in 1985. He lost his case, but was quoted as saying, 'I was up against the Nevada Gaming Commission, the Resort Association, the State Attorney General and the biggest law firm in Nevada – let's just say the deck was stacked.

'They want to keep me out because I win – it's as simple as that. Yet what I'm doing is not cheating. It's skill.'

Charles hung up on bet

Prince Charles will make a very good king one day – but he should think himself lucky he is never likely to need to make a living as a professional gambler. His track record so far is not too bright.

In 1981, Prince Charles and the then Labour Party leader, Michael Foot, were together at a dinner. Mr Foot predicted a Labour victory in the forthcoming General Election. Prince Charles disagreed. He said no party would have an overall majority, and backed his opinion to the tune of a bottle of fine claret.

Mr Foot lost the election by a landslide, but won the royal wager – and HRH duly paid up, by sending round a bottle of claret to Mr Foot's home.

The next recorded instance of the Prince's gambling instinct emerging was during the tour of Australia in 1985 when HRH presented the trophy for that country's biggest race, the Melbourne Cup.

Handing over the trophy to winning jockey, Pat Hyland, the Prince said, 'I will excuse the fact that he beat the horse I put my money on by a very short head.'

Soccer it to me

Arranging to take the largest soccer bet ever struck seemed like a good idea at the time – but it ruined the season for me.

At the start of season 1985/86, I laid the *Daily Star* a bet on which they stood to win £1,000,000 if four footballing eventualities took place. For the *Star* to collect (and me to lose my job!) one football league club had to set a new record number of wins in its division, one club had to score 100 league goals in the first or second division; one player had to score forty goals in forty-two league matches, and one player had to score six goals in a league match.

As Manchester United in the first and Reading in the third divisions both set off at a cracking pace, my nerves began to fray. But towards the end of the season it finally became clear that we weren't going to have to pay out, and I was able to breathe a sigh of relief! . . .

. . . The 1986 World Cup finals involved me in controversy when I persuaded my company to ignore Maradona's 'handball' goal in the England v. Argentina match which officially ended 1–2, and to refund stakes to all those punters who bet on the game to be drawn.

And Maradona himself fell foul of a World Cup bet – announcing that he'd wager his gold Cartier watch on Italy beating France – but his time was up when they lost!

When he was a boy, superstar golfer Lee Trevino used to earn pocket money by taking bets on his ability to hit a golf ball with a pop bottle.

Party to a
winning wager

I was in my office during the last General Election campaign when a prominent SDP/Liberal Alliance representative came on to the telephone to enquire of our political expert, 'How much money would it take to cut our price as 100/1 outsiders to a price which is far shorter?' He said he was making the enquiry because certain members of the Alliance seriously felt that their long odds would suggest to some of their voters or would-be voters that they had no chance of winning and hence encourage those people to vote for one of the other parties!

Labour politician Ossie O'Brien supported this theory when he attacked pundits for making 'unrealistic suggestions that the SDP is forging ahead' in his Darlington constituency. 'You seem to be basing it not on scientific opinion polls,' he said, 'but on the odds being placed by people like William Hill. If we had a whip-round – and I will be prepared to contribute – and put a sufficient bet on we would change the odds instantly.'

And he was right, of course.

Not that the bookies are always right – ask Peter Tatchell who was well beaten in a bitter Bermondsey by-election campaign a couple of years ago, but who said during the campaign, 'I'm feeling on top of the world. I did thirty push-ups this morning and the bookies make me 3/1 on.'

Harold Wilson, too, apparently still has nightmares about the General Election he lost when both the pollsters and the bookies made him a certainty.

According to the *Guinness Book of Records*, the highest-ever General Election bet was £90,000 to win £20,000 for the Conservatives to return the most MPs in the 1983 General Election (of course, they did). Potentially the biggest winning election bet was the £5,000 staked by

Frank Egerton at odds of 200/1 (he'd have won a million) that his Centre Party would win the next General Election. It didn't.

Hottest election favourites ever were the Tories in 1983, and on Monday, 6 June of that year the *Sun*'s front page headline was 'No More Bets On Maggie'. I was quoted as explaining that William Hill had closed their book on the election because 'if we were still offering odds they would be 1/9. So if someone put £100,000 on them to win he wouldn't make a single penny because of betting tax.'

Popping on a bet

Perhaps the biggest-ever bet on a pop record was £5,000, placed by Island Records in 1979 that the single by their new signing, trio U.S. of A., would reach the top ten.

Entitled '2/1 I Bet Ya', those were the odds the company took, and they were so confident that the cover design was based around a betting slip.

It flopped dismally.

Fans of teenybop idol Shakin' Stevens were more fortunate at Christmas, 1985 when they plunged large amounts of cash on their hero reaching the number one position by 25 December with his 'Merry Christmas Everyone'. So heavily did they back him that the odds shrunk from 25/1 to odds-on, displacing the hotly fancied Band Aid's 'Do They Know It's Christmas?' as favourite. The fans collected when the single hit the top in Christmas week.

Less fortunate was the group Space Cadet from Brighton, who bet that their first single would go gold – tin might have been more accurate! Also unlucky were the group Blue Nile, who backed themselves to put their debut album into the top five in 1984, and the Blackpool man who wanted £100 on a record about macho man Rambo hitting the number one slot.

They were all backing losers.

Taking the blinkers off

There was much rejoicing amongst punters in Greenock, Scotland in 1985 – they were finally allowed to read the racing pages of their daily papers!

Only then did the local public library finally end a practice, which had dated back to the nineteenth century, of blacking out all references to horse racing in the daily papers on display. Chief librarian Joy Monteith admitted, 'I'm absolutely mortified. The practice seems to have been carried on unthinkingly.'

A spokesman for the Libraries Association explained, 'The blacking out was an attempt to keep people away from gin palaces and racing. I must admit I thought it had stopped at least sixty years ago.'

The library janitor was entrusted with the task, using an ink pad and a roller to carry it out.

However, canny locals had long ago seen through it. Said a regular at the library, 'We had to hold them up to the light and read through the ink!'

Come on, old boy!

Punters who fancied the chances of Mollie in the 1935 Corinthian Plate Race at Baldoyle, Dublin were not so sure when they saw who was riding the filly – her owner, eighty-three-year-old Harry Beasley!

She finished unplaced.

And racegoers betting on Alike winning the 1929 Irish Grand National were delighted when their selection won – but how many of them, I wonder, were aware that Alike's jockey, Frank Wise, lost a leg and the tops of three fingers in the Great War!

A year after he'd won $4 million, a punter still hadn't claimed it! And officials of the Pennsylvania Lottery said that the money would be set aside to help the elderly.
It is the largest uncollected jackpot in history.

Finney's fun

One of Britain's finest actors, Albert Finney, was nearly lost to the thespian profession. By becoming a bookmaker he would have followed in the footsteps of his father and uncle, involved in the bookmaking business in Salford. But his acting abilities soon took him away from the betting trade.

However, he remains a racing enthusiast. On one afternoon, he was set to pay £25,000 for his fun. His colt, Synastry, was a declared runner in the legendary Kentucky Derby. Albert wanted to see the race, so he planned to purchase all the seats in the house at the theatre where he was playing, reimburse the bar for its loss of takings and buy six Concorde tickets to fly himself and his chums over to the States.

In the event, Synastry was sidelined through injury, so Albert saved his money, but he said, 'It's a shame. Kentucky would have been fun.'

Animal madness

What do cocks, dogs, rats and cage-birds have in common?

They were all frequently gambled upon in the mid-nineteenth century.

Cock fighting was big business in the gambling world for some time, and it is reported that in 1830 one of the greatest cocking matches ever took place when Lord Derby and the great game-fowl breeder Gilliver put up seven birds a side with 1,000 guineas on each separate stake and 5,000 on the match.

It was also a 'sport' in which reluctant losing punters were persuaded to pay up by a novel method – cock-pits were often equipped with cages, rather like large lobster pots, into which anyone unable to pay off a losing bet was 'persuaded' by the management. The cages were attached by a pulley to a roof beam, and once the punter was in he would be hoisted up to ceiling level!

Betting on contests between fighting-dogs, another cruel 'sport', was commonplace.

Ratting was also extremely popular and the creatures were caught and bred in profusion to supply the rat-pits where animals, usually either ferrets or bull-terriers, would be backed to kill a given number of rats within a certain time.

Jimmy Shaw, who ran a ratting house, was said to have as many as 2,000 rats on the premises at one time.

Rather a more gentle gamble could be had by training birds – starlings, blackbirds, thrushes, finches, linnets and night-ingales – to imitate a constantly repeated air or 'toy', whistled or played upon a pipe.

Sadly, some birds were blinded in the belief that they would sing better. Once trained they would be entered for 'julking' or bird-singing competitions in which they were set to compete against one another, with lively wagering taking place on the outcome.

Sel-lose Froggitt?

Actor Bill Maynard, well known for his TV role as the character Selwyn Froggitt, stood as an Independent Labour candidate at a by-election in March 1984.

So confident was he of doing well that he backed himself to the tune of £2,000 to poll over 1,500 votes, at odds of 5/2.

Agonizingly, he totalled 1,355.

A Bon bet

When Duran Duran singer Simon Le Bon completed the Whitbread Round The World Yacht Race in 1986, in third place in his boat *Drum*, the *Daily Mirror* revealed that someone had struck a bet of $4,000 that he would die during the race!

The *Mirror*'s Christina Appleyard reported, ' "Mind your own business," he said when asked who had bet $4,000 that he would die.'

By-election betting bonanza

The Brecon by-election in autumn, 1985 must take the biscuit as being the most gambling-oriented of all time.

Apart from the Conservative, who declared early in the campaign that he had no time for bookies or opinion polls, every other party put money on itself – with two famous politicians losing their gambling 'virginity'!

Those two were Liberal leader David Steel, who risked a whole fiver on his eventually triumphant candidate, Richard Livesey, and Labour's Dennis Healey who also broke the habit of a lifetime to stake a quid on his candidate.

Mr Roger Everest, the Independent Conservative, was so confident of success (he finished sixth) that he laid out enough to win himself £90,000, while Monster Raving Loony Party candidate Lord Sutch won his deposit back by wagering that he would poll over one hundred votes. His agent did even better – he won a bet struck at odds of 8/1 that he could place all seven candidates in the correct order in which they would finish.

Wogan's winning wager

Before he discovered TV, Terry Wogan had a popular radio show, a regular feature of which was a daily racing tip, Wogan's Wager. It was very popular with the bookies, so inconsistent was its success.

Until, that is, the day that a punter turned up at the bookies, tipped £20,000 cash on to the counter and asked for it all to be plonked on the nose of Wogan's Wager that day – 'Whatever it is'!

After ringing the BBC to discover the name of the animal, the bet was placed – and duly won at 5/2.

Next day the punter came back, collecting his £45,800 profit in cash – and leaving £25,000 of it on the counter again for that day's selection. It bolted in at 2/1.

That won him another £45,500 – and he repeated the performance a third time.

This time the nag galloped in at 9/2, and the punter had earned over a quarter of a million pounds in three days.

Tony Fairbairn, director of the Racing Information Bureau who provided Wogan's selections, says that no one ever knew who the punter was. Nor did he send so much as a postcard of thanks to Wogan and the team responsible for his fortune!

Leaping Tom

Tom Scott, described as a 'popular local sportsman', caused a sensation in Liverpool in 1870 when accepting and winning a wager by jumping, without a horse, one complete circuit of the Grand National course.

Try again, Ref!

International Rugby Union referee, Alan Hosie, still blushes when he recalls his most embarrassing moment.

It came when Alan, a member of Hillhead Rugby Club, was about to leave his dressing room to make his international debut, reffing the England versus Ireland match at Twickenham. He received a pre-match telegram, but was too nervous to open it and passed it to English Rugby Union secretary Bob Weighill to read it for him.

The telegram read, 'Your bet of £200 on Ireland is accepted. Signed William Hill.'

Alan says the heat from his red face could have melted the brass necks of his Hillhead pals who sent it!

Secretary Troulla Michaelides, thirty, of Melbourne, Australia, sent a bet of £150 to a London bookmaker, wagering that she would marry Prince Andrew during 1984.

Punter Paul turns punk

Thirty-six-year-old company boss Paul Tremayne of Leeds won £250 of bets when he adopted a punk-style Mohican haircut in 1983.

Paul donated his winnings to charity and said, 'It changed my view of the punks who ask me for jobs.'

Down to earth bet

Several years ago an American Skylab was due to return to earth from space – but no one was quite sure where it was likely to land.

A bus driver from Newquay in Cornwall wrote to me, enclosing a pound note. 'The American space laboratory, Skylab, is falling out of the sky, they say. My £1 says it will fall on the Western National Bus/Coach Garage in Tolcarne Road, Newquay – or at least part of it.

'Before quoting odds, be warned – we get all the unwanted old wrecks here!

'PS. Please pay my next of kin if I happen to be here when it arrives!'

Naturally,
a historic bet

The lady at the Natural History Museum kept her cool when I rang her and said, 'If I were to tell you I'd found a dinosaur alive and well would you be prepared to verify my claim?'

'Certainly,' she said, without hesitation.

Which was just as well, because I'd just laid punter Mr N. Burroughs from Wiltshire a £10 bet at odds of 100/1 that he couldn't produce a live dinosaur or conclusive proof of the current existence of one before the end of March 1991.

I'd spoken on the phone to Mr Burroughs who, whilst extremely confident of winning the wager, wasn't telling just why he thought he was on a winner.

No doubt he'll be dragging a large carcass up to my office very shortly!

Out for the count

Boxer Len McLean came up with a knockout idea to win himself some cash. He'd back himself to the tune of £15,000 to win his next fight.

However, there was one small snag: Len, who boxed on unlicensed shows, didn't have £15,000 to stake. So he asked his bank manager to lend him the money.

'The manager had seen me fight before and thought the bet was a good thing,' he said. 'He was at the ringside and even bet on me himself.'

Which wasn't a good idea, for thirty-two-year-old Len was taking on 6′7″ Cliff Field – who thrashed him in five rounds.

Shortly after, in April 1982, Len appeared in the London Bankruptcy Court as a direct result of that wager and his defeat, with debts of £8,350 to his name.

The bank manager was sacked.

Luck be a
lady tonight!

Illegal gambling was proving tremendously popular in Marlene Pearson's tavern in Illinois, and the local police chief couldn't quite understand why – until he discovered what the punters were gambling for.

Forty-five-year-old Marlene was offering the services of prostitutes as winnings in her illegal games of chance, reported the local law.

Punters paid a stake of one or two dollars to select lucky numbers. Said Rudy Gandolfi, police chief of the small town of Oglesby where it was all happening early in 1986, 'I've heard of salamis and fishing reels and all sorts of prizes in illegal tavern gambling – but I've never heard of girls before. We found it pretty hard to believe.'

Di hands out a winner

Pools punter Dale Gould, twenty-seven, of Shropshire shook hands with Princess Diana when she opened a leisure centre near his home in March 1986. He then rushed off home to fill in his coupon with the same hand. 'It seemed such a good omen that I wouldn't wash when I got home in case I washed the luck away.'

He didn't. He won £222,000 with his entry.

A Lee-ding
punter

Former England international footballer Francis Lee has
always been a keen punter. He told how he and a colleague
bought a horse between them.

'As a youngster I had always fancied owning a racehorse
but I wouldn't have one until I could afford one. Then,
when I was at Derby, Rod Thomas and I bought one for
£13 each! One day we had an accumulator bet for £26 and
they all won. We picked up two and a half grand.

'So we bought this horse, Clydebank.

'I remember the first time we really fancied it. He was
running at Chepstow, but it was a Saturday and we were
playing Wolves at home, so we couldn't go. We needed to
win to go top of the League.

'That morning the assistant manager Des Anderson
came in and told me and Rod, "I've got some very bad
news." We thought, bloody hell, the horse has broken a
leg, but instead he told us that the match had been
abandoned.

'We said "What a shame!" And if we had won we would
have gone top of the League! But really it was all we could
do to stop laughing.

'We raced down to Chepstow and watched the horse
scoot in at 8/1. I remember thinking "Christ, this is easy."'

The best policy

William Murphy made himself a dollar millionaire by winning a lottery he hadn't even entered.

The twenty-eight-year-old Canadian found a lottery ticket in March 1986 inside a wallet which he picked up on a Montreal street.

He returned the wallet and kept the lottery ticket. 'I figured it might be good for $10 or so,' he said.

It turned out to be good for $7 million (£3.3 million)!

So unemployed Murphy set off to East Montreal, knocked on the door of Jean-Guy Lavigeur and told him, 'You're a millionaire.'

Once the message had sunk in (Murphy spoke only English, Lavigeur only French), Lavigeur decided that such honesty deserved a reward – and gave Murphy $1 million.

Sir,

At the outset I offer my most sincere and humble salutations to your good self.

I beg to submit the following:

It is my sincere faith from out of diagrammatic proof that man along with not less than 10,000 people will go and reside at one of the planets on or before 2050 AD. I am ready to place this fact for a challenge and a bet. I am ready to deposit R.500 towards this bet. May I receive a favourable reply from your respectable self?

Thanking you.

Yours Sincerely,

Bill's wild bet

Legendary Wild-West character Wild Bill Hickok loved to gamble and thought he was on a winner when he was dealt two pairs, aces and eights, during a poker game.

As Hickok moved to play the hand he was shot in the back of the head, and ever since that particular set of cards has been known as Dead Man's Hand.

Q. **Which gambling game is French scientist Blaise Pascal credited with inventing in 1655 during a monastic retreat?**
A. **Roulette.**

So who's crazy?

A syndicate of hospital staff from Wiltshire who landed a record £1,017,890 win from Littlewoods Pools in 1986 had allowed psychiatric patients to pick the winning numbers for them. And pools punters have been known to dream up all sorts of plans for spotting winners – some of them with amazing success.

Doris Binfield of Nottingham scooped £500,000. She bought a 45p bingo set and threw the numbered balls down on to her kitchen floor, marking off the numbers that came up.

Lorry driver Eddie Brown of Liverpool won over £188,000 by marking down tram numbers on his coupon.

Ray Fairfax used the medium-wave stations on his car radio to pick winning numbers – he twiddled the knob at random and divided by ten the wavelengths he landed on. Crazy? He won £32,000.

Ken Charlesworth bought a toy roulette wheel and let that pick his numbers – £120,000 worth!

Eric Birks had a great system of using people's ages. The trouble was he couldn't remember how old his wife was. Forty-three, he thought, and put down that number, duly collecting £138,000 – after which she told him she was forty-two!

Fred Campbell figured lightning might just strike twice – so he filled in all the numbers which had come up as draws the previous week. He won over half a million!

Lawrence Freedman tried a trick on friends and told them he'd won the pools, offering to sell his coupon for £100. No one fell for it and a few days later Lawrence found out he *had* won – £300,000.

Accountant Kenneth Grimes from Hampshire checked his coupon in March 1972 and decided he had nothing to come. Wrong! He was the first-ever £500,000 winner. And former policewoman Phyllis Bell from Doncaster kept the pools representative outside for an hour because she thought he was a con-man. He wasn't – he'd come to tell her she'd won £109,000!

But few of these winners emulated fifty-five-year-old Lewis Gould of Kidderminster, a 1986 pools winner of £110,000 who promptly went out and signed on the dole!

Hairy madness

Two members of one of Britain's favourite groups, Madness, began to grow their hair at the same time.

Said Lee Thompson to Chris Foreman, 'I bet I can grow my hair for longer than you without having it cut.'

Said Chris Foreman, 'Oh no you can't, and what's more, I bet I can go for a whole year without having it cut.'

As *Top of the Pops* viewers can confirm, the two became hairier and hairier until, after six months, Thompson gave up the struggle and fled screaming to the hairdressers.

Foreman, however, was made of sterner stuff – he made it right through to the year's end without facing the chop. Then, having won the bet, he gratefully had a close crop.

'There was no actual stake involved,' explained a spokesman from Zarjazz, Madness' record company. 'It was a sportsman's bet and Chris considers that the principle at stake was sufficient incentive.'

First among betters?

Deputy chairman of the Conservative Party and best-selling author Jeffrey Archer was prepared to bet £1,000 on the outcome of the 1986 London Marathon.

He was reported in the *Observer* as wagering this sum that Frank Marshall and Kathleen Kennedy, the producers of such Oscar-winning films as *E.T.* and *Raiders of the Lost Ark*, would not complete the course in under three hours. The terms of the bet were that if the pair failed to run the Marathon in this time, they would then donate £1,000 to a charity; but if they were successful, Archer would donate the money himself.

And they were successful. Mr Archer told me, 'Frank Marshall did indeed complete the course in under three hours, and I will be donating my stake to the Great Ormond Street hospital.'

Under holy orders!

The Church of England's first racehorse went into training during the 1986 flat season – with her vicar owner confessing to putting a few bob on her.

St Wendred, a two-year-old filly, was given for a year to the parish of St Martins, Exning, near Newmarket, by a local trainer.

Reverend Cedric Catton, who was registered as her owner, wanted her to run in liturgical colours. They came up with the colours used for altar dressing, red, purple, green and white.

When Reverend Catton was asked whether he would bet on the filly, he said, 'I think you can say that we will be supporting her in the usual way.' But punters didn't have a prayer when the filly made her debut – she finished last.

Plaice betting?

In the early sixties, when betting shops had just become legal, one of the success stories was that of fifty-year-old Jumbo Howard who opened up a shop – on his Lowestoft-based North Sea fishing trawler!

Ash cash for Ian

England's cricketers were delighted to win the Ashes from the Australians in the 1985 series – particularly Ian Botham, who won a £10,000 bet in the process.

In the second test Botham ripped through the Aussies' batting to take five wickets – and then revealed that he'd won himself £5,000 from his millionaire business partner Tim Hudson.

Explained Botham, 'Tim bet me £5,000 I couldn't take five wickets in the Aussie first innings. I'm not a great gambler but I just couldn't resist it.'

Then Hudson revealed that Ian had decided not to claim his winnings – 'I was ready to fork out £5,000 at the close of play but Ian immediately said that he wanted the cash on England to win the series' (at even money). 'I only hope our wager helps win back the Ashes.'

It did.

On the spot!

Albert Wright of Leeds claims to have played a domino match for the largest stake ever – £25,000.

Albert told his friend, betting shop manager Ken Wilson, 'Early in 1947 I bought two tickets for the Irish Sweepstakes but, whilst playing dominoes in the pub for half a crown (12½p), I became financially embarrassed and had to sell the tickets in order to stay in the game.

'Needless to say, one of the tickets drew Caughoo, which won £25,000 for the two chaps who bought my tickets!'

Punters in the pink

Keen budgerigar breeders have been backing themselves to produce their impossible dream – a pink budgerigar.

Of all the billions of budgerigars brought into this world, not one of them has yet been proved to be pink.

Not that breeders haven't tried to land the 100/1 odds available from William Hill.

Arthur Bracey, an official of the British Budgerigar Society and the man responsible for verifying claims, says, 'We've had people bring us birds covered in brick dust, birds who've been dyed and birds who've been rubbed against iodine blocks.'

Mr Bracey also related how one audacious attempt to con the adjudicators by means of food colouring was only exposed after they kept the bird long enough for it to moult, revealing its true colours!

To land the odds, three-quarters of the body area must be pink. *Observer* columnist Sue Arnold suggested crossing a very small pink flamingo with a very large budgie!

Winning royalties

In 1977 under a front-page lead headline, 'Bookies Ban Anne's Baby' in the *Sunday Mirror*, I explained why my company were not accepting bets on what sex Princess Anne's forthcoming baby would be. 'Some people think it is in bad taste, so we aren't getting involved.'

How times change.

Just a few years later Princess Diana had joined the Royal Family. Suddenly attitudes changed greatly. When it was announced that she was pregnant the betting interest was so great that we were virtually forced to open a book on the sex of the baby.

Then we bet on what the name of the baby would be – with George as favourite.

A sudden rush of money for the name William, which reduced the price from 20/1 to 7/2, proved to be inspired, and rumours were rife that 'inside knowledge' was involved.

Those punters who opted for and placed cash on names like Elvis, Bjorn, Adolf and Truck (the last name placed by a DJ in Phoenix, Arizona in case the Royals decided to name their first born after a local basketball hero!) lost their cash.

Second time round the betting on the sex of the baby suddenly hit the front pages of every tabloid newspaper when on Tuesday, 3 April 1984 we had to close the book on Diana giving birth to twins after taking a sudden flurry of large bets of up to £750 at 50/1. Once again, the papers suspected a royal 'leak' of information.

The information was inaccurate, however, and Prince Henry, known as Harry, duly arrived, winning us a fortune as not one single punter backed either Henry or Harry to be the name.

One royal bet did cost the bookies a great deal of money. On 14 November 1973 a horse called Royal Mark was running. Nothing odd about that? Well, there wouldn't have been had it not been running – in the Royal Wedding Handicap Chase at Windsor – on the day that Princess Anne was marrying Captain Mark Phillips.

Inevitably Royal Mark won, at odds of 11/10.

Q. What was the amount of the wager made by Phileas Fogg that he could go 'Around The World In Eighty Days' in the Jules Verne novel of that title?
A. £20,000.

Wedded bliss

Annette Barrios, twenty-three and on her honeymoon in Las Vegas, not unnaturally fancied an early night. But her husband persuaded her to stay up for a while longer and to have a go on a slot machine.

At 2.30 a.m. Annette, a £90-a-week hospital worker from Santa Paula, won $1,000,000.

'I'm going to trust in the Lord to show us how to spend the money,' she said.

A funny thing happened at the bookies (3)

The young couple perched precariously on a stool in the Swindon betting shop were doing what comes naturally to the male and female of the species – sort of an each-way double of their own. But the manager had to ask them tactfully to desist when outraged punters complained – they couldn't hear the race commentaries because the couple were getting so carried away! . . .

. . . The counter clerk in a London West End shop was approached by a bus conductor carrying a long list of bets 'from the lads at the garage'. As she rang up the bets on the till the conductor became agitated. 'Hurry up, luv, I've got a bus outside with forty passengers on it.' He had, too . . .

. . . A punter in a Doncaster shop had a wooden leg and had to lean up against the counter to write his bets out. When another punter came in with his Jack Russell terrier the dog and the leg had an unfortunate encounter which finished up with the leg somewhat damper than it had previously been!

Punting for ports

The first recorded lottery in England took place in 1569 to raise money for the repair of the Cinque Ports. There were 400,000 lots and the prizes were in plate, tapestry and money.

During the next hundred years, lotteries were promoted for public purposes: in aid of English plantations in Virginia (1612); to finance schemes for bringing fresh water to London (1627); to repair the damage done to the fishing fleet by the Spaniards (1640); for the ransom of English slaves in Tunis and for poor and maimed soldiers (1660).

By 1776 there was an annual state lottery, which survived until 1826.

Abroad, in more recent times, state controlled lotteries have paid for the building of the Sydney Opera House and helped to finance the Montreal Olympic Games.

Fishing for winners

There's a gentleman working in the Federal Department of Fisheries in Nigeria who is convinced that I know in advance the results of all the football matches played in this country!

And he's not the only one – on average I receive a letter a month from that country demanding that I let them in on the secret.

Quite why they believe I am privy to this useful information I cannot say – but listen to what the Fisheries Department man (whose name was illegible) wanted from me: 'Five draws, starting from week ten until the end of the

English season' – but in case I failed to grasp the point of a bookie providing punters with winners (even if it were possible!) he added, 'The business will be done strictly on a credit basis – and a substantial part of my business will be sent to you.'

One of my other correspondents guessed that I had 'secret keys to draws which I can arrange to buy from you. If, on the alternative, you are not in possession of the keys would you therefore be good enough to direct me to such addresses.'

Then he confided why he wanted these mysterious keys: 'To enable me to make a fortune.'

Well, I'm afraid I couldn't help them but I remember someone who may once have been able to – that legendary gentleman who used to advertise regularly during the sixties on Radio Luxembourg, that he could tip the results of soccer matches, and who used to sign off as 'Mr Horace Batchelor of Keynsham, that's K,E,Y,N,S,H,A,M . . .'

Do you want the good news or . . . ?

Guatemalan-born Julio Morales, twenty-three, won the equivalent of a million pounds in the Californian State lottery – later the same day he was deported as an illegal immigrant! He kept the money, though . . .

. . . Conservative MP Toby Jessel was delighted to win a raffle prize – until he found it was a signed photo of Labour leader Neil Kinnock . . .

. . . Fifty-five-year-old Londoner Joe Racsis had £2 to his name. He staked it on an accumulator and won £800.

Minutes after he had collected his winnings, he was mugged – and the lot was stolen.

Larry raises the bet

Harmonica player Larry Adler is willing to bet £1,000 against proof of the paranormal being produced.

In a letter to satirical magazine *Private Eye* in 1985, Adler mentioned that in his autobiography, *It Ain't Necessarily So*, he offered £1,500 for proof that anyone has levitated, before adding, 'No takers so far. I'll go further – £1,000, or a 2/1 bet, £2,000 to £1,000, take your choice, for verifiable proof of any paranormal phenomenon of any kind.

'My only condition: a professional stage magician, such as James Randi, must be present.'

Eight days a week

Seen recently in the *London Standard* newspaper:
'Croupier (roulette) to work in a non-gambling situation seven or eight nights a week.'